GOD USES ORDINARY PEOPLE

The Autobiography / Biography of Danniebelle Hall

Danniebelle Hall with Cynthia Hall Philpot

Forever Danniebelle

Copyright © 2023 by Danniebelle Hall with Cynthia Hall Philpot

All rights reserved.

No portion of this book may be reproduced in any form without written permission from the publisher or author, except as permitted by U.S. copyright law.

This publication is designed to provide accurate and authoritative information in regard to the subject matter covered. It is sold with the understanding that neither the author nor the publisher is engaged in rendering legal, investment, accounting or other professional services. While the publisher and author have used their best efforts in preparing this book, they make no representations or warranties with respect to the accuracy or completeness of the contents of this book and specifically disclaim any implied warranties of merchantability or fitness for a particular purpose. No warranty may be created or extended by sales representatives or written sales materials. The advice and strategies contained herein may not be suitable for your situation. You should consult with a professional when appropriate. Neither the publisher nor the author shall be liable for any loss of profit or any other commercial damages, including but not limited to special, incidental, consequential, personal, or other damages.

ISBN 979-8-9881793-1-3 (Hardback Edition)
ISBN 979-8-9881793-2-0 (EBook)

Library of Congress Control Number: 2023908002

Unless otherwise noted, Scripture quotations are from the *King James Version* of the Holy Bible.

Just Ordinary People. Lyrics by Danniebelle Hall. Copyright © 1977 Birdwing Music (ASCAP) Danniebelle Music (ASCAP) Universal Music - Brentwood Benson Publ. (ASCAP) All rights reserved. Used by permission.

Front cover photo courtesy of David J. Pavol (www.pavol.com)

Book design courtesy of Amy Miller (www.amykmillerdesign.com)

Author and back cover copy by Tim Dillinger-Curenton

Author Cynthia Hall Philpot photo by All2Good Productions (www.all2goodproductions.com)

Printed and bound in the United States of America

First printing, 2023

COPYRIGHT

Forever Danniebelle
336 Georgia Avenue STE 106 #164
North Augusta, SC 29841

www.danniebelle.com

*This book is dedicated to my children,
Charlotte, Charles "Timothy," and Cynthia.*

*My "GrannyBelles,"
Trinese, Charisse, Lance, Cameron, Cedric, Vanessa, Michelle, Melinda, Jaden, and Jordan.*

*My "Great-GrannyBelles,"
DeAndre, Davian, Marlee, Charlotte, Mikey, Edmond, Luna Belle, and Brandon.*

*May you always hide God's Word in your heart (Psalm 119:11).
As you read it every day, you will grow.
To know Christ is to love Him."*

~yours, Danniebelle

Contents

Foreword	VI
Preface	IX
Introduction	XIII
Prologue	XIV
1. Childhood	1
2. Early Family Life	12
3. The Danniebelles	22
4. Andrae Crouch & The Disciples	31
5. On Her Own	38
6. The Cankerworm	50
7. Restoration	60
8. The Final Years	73
9. Letters From Danniebelle	83
10. Well Done	98
Acknowledgements	103

Foreword

Danniebelle Hall was born on October 6, 1938. She was an "unlikely" prodigy. "Unlikely" because odds were that she would never step foot on a national platform, simply due to her background and circumstances.

Her parents, William and Danniebell Jones, weren't well-off and had eight kids to raise. They could barely afford to invest in piano lessons, and there were times when Danniebelle went to bed hungry because there wasn't much to eat. At points in her young life, hand-me-down clothes were the best she had.

Nonetheless, she was a prodigy. Her ear and piano training began informally, at the tender age of three, in her hometown church, and she soon blossomed into a skillful musician and songwriter. However, the musical prowess of Danniebelle was arguably superseded by her heart for God and people. That's the secret that this book reveals.

While fans are always fascinated by the musical output of artists and musicians, Danniebelle's story strikes a deeper chord.

FOREWORD

Growing up in the mid-1940s, life wasn't easy for her. Nearly a quarter century later, the Civil Rights movement declared, "I'm Black, and I'm Proud!" And almost eight decades before the "Me Too!" movement elevated the voices of women. In fact, "Me Too" didn't become a "thing" until 2006, six years after Danniebelle waved goodbye to this world.

So...How did Danniebelle make an impact? By passionately pursuing her life's mission, which was to love and minister to "Ordinary People." She had an unconquerable zeal, an inextinguishable courage, and an unyielding faith. These qualities propelled her over, through, and past the obstacles that life threw her way. And there were many. But she ministered no matter what and no matter where. She blessed people when she felt "mountain-top" good, as well as when she battled in the valleys of emotional and physical challenges. Contrary to the industry trappings of entourage and superficiality, Danniebelle exuded a down-home, authentic genuineness. Music was her gift to minister and share the love of Jesus with others.

Interestingly, Danniebelle was known for her warmth and hospitality. She never met a stranger, and strangers left her presence feeling like old friends, no matter if the encounter was at a conference, concert, or a one-on-one conversation. People felt like they had a personal invitation to be in Danniebelle's living room—the place where she would sit at the piano and pour out for the world what God had poured into her spirit.

I personally experienced Danniebelle. The first time I recall her singing was at an event populated with over 200 Gospel legends sponsored by Bill Gaither. Danniebelle sang "Through It All." It was amazing! The second recollection I'll share was at the Gospel Music Workshop of America. It was one of those late-night musicals where you struggle to stay awake, and at a point, everything sounds like a lullaby.

GMWA founder and president, Rev. James Cleveland, had announced that this late-night musical's special guest was Ms. Danniebelle Hall. Well, that was it for me! I had to be there! Sleepy, groggy, and worn-out, it didn't matter.

I will never forget it. It was the early days of my business endeavors with *Gospel Today Magazine*, and I was there on a wing and a prayer. I was teetering on the edge of throwing in the towel and giving up on the Magazine. That night, at the conclusion of the marathon of singers, choirs, groups, and announcers, Danniebelle went to the piano and began singing. At some point, she got to the song I needed to hear... "Ordinary People." She sang, *"God uses people just like me and you...who are willing to do as He commands."*

That night, with tears streaming down my face, I went to my room and promised God to "do as He commanded."

Thank you, Danniebelle!
Dr. Teresa Hairston
Founder/Publisher Emeritus, *Gospel Today Magazine*
Founder, Gospel Heritage Foundation

Preface

You may know Danniebelle Hall as a great artist or as an incredible songwriter. Perhaps you remember witnessing one of Danniebelle's solo performances, or you experienced her ministry as a lead vocalist with Andrae Crouch's Disciples. However, I am honored to call Danniebelle Hall "Mom." I'm Cynthia Hall Philpot, Danniebelle's youngest daughter and the youngest of her three children.

Along with my siblings, Charles (aka Timmy) and Charlotte (the best big sister and brother in the world), this book is presented in tribute to our mother's life and legacy. Without their support and encouragement, I couldn't have completed this book. They understood that it was my assignment to finish writing Mom's story, which she started before she passed in 2000.

This book is grounded in our love and faith in Jesus Christ, which our parents and grandparents taught us at a young age. It is the glue that continues to bind us together.

We were raised in Northern California. San Jose, to be exact. Charlotte and Timmy still live in Cali, but I moved to South Carolina in 1994. A few months before Mom passed, she sent me a cassette tape with the words "Prophecy In Jacksonville" written across the top. She said, "Cynthia, I want you to listen to this tape. I believe he is talking about you. I want you to "finish writing my book," I thought, "oooh, okaaaay Mommy, sure - I can do that!?" I listened to the tape of an unknown preacher speaking a prophecy to my mother. This is some of what he said:

"Danniebelle, the Lord spoke to me (are you ready?) The Lord spoke to me and said that he is going to relaunch, not your career, but your ministry ...the Lord is going to launch your ministry afresh.

They'll think that they're just going to honor one of the old timers, and they do not know, says the Lord, that in the honoring of an old timer, they're inviting the spirit of revival to come in, says the Lord. For I am going to anoint you with a fresh anointing, and I will give you those who were your friends and compatriots, and they shall be revived, and I will reinvigorate you and the ministry that I will give you.

*Take the manuscripts out of the mothballs. Take them out and make them relevant and fresh again, and I will publish it, and I will put it out there, and there will be **a generation** who didn't know your music who will know My Name, and then I'll introduce them to your music, and I'll give you a new name, says the Lord.*

The Lord says that as you do this, there's a daughter, a flesh and blood daughter that the Spirit of the Lord is gonna reach out to, and she's gonna return to her calling. And it's a sign from the Lord for you — the healing power of God. Folks, lift your hands and say Amen to the word of the Lord - **Hallelujah!***"*

Our mother went on to glory on December 28th, 2000.

Why then, are you getting this story some 20+ years later? When given an assignment, the student must be prepared in order to complete the assignment. The student is also given a due date to complete the assignment. In this case, the due date given for this assignment was "in God's own timing."

It is 'for such a time as this' that I present our mother's story to you.

This book is both autobiographical and biographical. Mom left manuscripts in notebooks and cassette tapes about her life. In transcribing her story, I learned so much more about her. I always knew my mom loved good food, and was hilarious! Oh...the laughs!

Most of all, I learned about her steadfast love for God. She loved to share the gospel of Jesus Christ with others and praise and worship God. She longed to know Him better and serve Him with her whole heart. Her songs and ministry reflect her love for God and His unconditional love for us. Anyone who saw her in concert could see that she would simply serenade the Father through praise and worship and invite us to do the same.

Unfortunately, there were parts of her story that she did not finish. To capture some of the missing pieces, I had the pleasure of interviewing several of Mom's family members and friends.

Although our Mom was a renowned artist, she didn't have a music career. She had a ministry.

The purpose of this book is three-fold.
1. To share my mother's story, impact, and history in the gospel music world.

2. To share my mother's ministry with a generation who didn't know her music.

3. To finish an assignment (Look Mommy, I finished cleaning up my room!)

ALL for the Glory of God!

~Cynthia Hall Philpot

Introduction

In this book, you will learn more about my Mom, just like I did. As you read her story, in her own words *(which are italicized)*, as well as the narrative that has been carefully and accurately assembled from sources that include her siblings, family, and friends, you will undoubtedly be inspired by her commitment and courage. ~Cynthia

One day, I know this little book will be worth a lot, both to my children and the people whose lives I've touched all over the world.

My imperfections are recorded here for me to review as long as I live and for my friends who thought they knew me, but as they read this, they will realize they didn't know all of me. And in spite of what they knew, they still loved me.

My whole thing in life and loving has been, "I want to be the best friend you've ever had, and if I can't help you, I don't ever want to hurt you."
~Danniebelle

Prologue

"At the end of this session, I want each of you to go to your room without saying a word to anyone. When you get to your room, take a tablet and jot down areas of your life that seem to be giving you difficulty. Write things out in detail, and then spend some time in silent prayer asking the Lord to deal with those areas and when you are finished, tear the paper up."

I listened as attentively as I could to our moderator, trying to remember what he was telling us well enough to be able to follow his instructions. Giving him all of my attention wasn't the easiest thing that night. Our friend, Marion Nichols, had invited the Danniebelles to a Campus Crusade Weekend Lay Institute. Because I was the group's leader, most of my attention had been focused on getting to Arrowhead Springs and performing, so we could make as good an impression as possible. I definitely wasn't tuned into what the Holy Spirit was trying to do in us.

How did I get a group anyway? I mean, I never had any aspirations to be a leader, and organizing just wasn't a part of my nature. The epitome of success in my mind would have been to be a pianist or organist for some itinerant evangelist. I didn't really care which evangelist. I just wanted to play and *travel. Piano was my main thing. I studied for about six years. The fact that I was even able to take piano lessons was a miracle in and of itself, but more about that later.*

So there we were, the Danniebelles, at the very beginning of what promised to be a worthwhile ministry. I must admit I suffered from delusions of grandeur at first. If most musicians/would-be artists were honest, they'd have to admit that at one time or another, almost everyone has experienced similar feelings.

My mind kept thinking, 'We really have a tough [great] sound. Boy, oh boy, if only [so-and-so] could hear us, I know they'd be impressed, and all kinds of opportunities would open to us.' I was right...up to a point. Truth was, we did have a good sound, but more importantly, the Holy Spirit had to help us get our heads in the right place and put our priorities in the proper perspective so we could effectively minister to people's needs.

I had the notion that I had to barge in and break down the doors instead of trusting the Lord to provide for us. He was dealing with my attitude that night, but I was unaware of what was happening.

It seems that the more traumatic a person's life has been, the more interesting it is to others to read about. I used to wish that I could give a testimony of how God delivered me from a life of drug addiction and violence and how He snatched me from degradation and lifted me out of the muck and mire. That's always more sensational. But instead, a constant changing and development of certain attitudes have characterized my life. I'm learning that the attitudinal level of life seems to be the weightier side of the scale with the Lord. He seems to be more concerned with dealing with our temperament and emotions rather than with what I call external symptoms of internal turmoil. We tend to miss the subtle reshaping and transformational work of the Holy Spirit. He deals with us as we open ourselves to Him. He very gently opens our eyes to areas of our lives that were previously closed.

As I sat there, half listening to what was being said, I began to wonder if the moderator was out of his wits. I knew he must have been if he thought we, seven women, were going to observe one minute of silence, not to mention an hour or more. Talking was like an involuntary reaction with us. You can believe seven black women always have a topic for discussion, and when all else fails, we could rely on "playing the dozens" and laugh at each other for hours.

I remember one time at Mount Hermon Christian Conference Center, we laughed at one thing after another all night long. Years later, one of the members of the group met a woman, and as Jimmye identified herself as one of the Danniebelles, the woman sort of half-smiled and said, "Oh yes, I do remember you all! I stayed in the cabin next to yours at Mount Hermon some years ago, and ever since then, I've wanted to know what in the world was so funny that you girls were laughing loud enough and long enough to keep me, my husband, and my child awake all night?" By that time, the half smile had slid off the woman's face, and Jimmye had to think up some excuse for us.

Faced with the verifiably impossible task of remaining silent, I walked back to our room, trying to quickly think of what needed to be dealt with. If I'd hurry up and think about it, all I'd have to do when I got to the room would be to scribble a couple of hasty lines on a little piece of paper and observe a moment of silent prayer, tear up the paper, and hop into bed. 'Actually,' I thought, 'I'm O.K. There really isn't that much for the Holy Spirit to help me with. I know I love everybody, or do I? What about that sister that seemed so cold toward me? Why couldn't I warm up to her?' I explained to myself that any coldness that existed was on her part because I knew I didn't have a cold bone in my body. Besides, if she wanted to act that way toward me, I didn't really need her love. She was the one that had deliberately excluded me. Like the time she didn't invite me to one of her annual dinners. And how about those scrutinizing looks she'd given me? I know my clothes weren't as good as hers, but did she have to look at me like that?

The more I thought about each of her bad points, the more she loomed higher and higher as a mountainous ogre. And the bigger she got, the more enraged I became at not being able to overlook her. Then a very tiny quiet thought edged its way to the front of my mind. 'What had I ever done to her to make her know that I loved and appreciated her? Had I ever assessed her worth to me? Was I so consumed by a desire for her to accept me that I had overlooked the fact that she, too, had needs?'

That night, in that room with six other women, surrounded by an almost deafening silence, I really heard myself, and as I looked inside of this 'O.K.' person. I saw a very selfish person that craved acceptance so much. My basic problem was the inability to accept myself as a worthwhile person.

I had grown up in a church that really laid into the scripture in Rom. 12:3 (KJV), let not a man think more highly of himself than he ought to think. The older people in the church took it as their personal obligation to see to it that none of the young people would get lifted up in pride. Over and over, they drilled into us, "You are nothing. You are nothing!" All flesh is grass and withers away (1 Pet. 1:24). You are nothing. A few years of that, and you actually believe that *you're nothing. Most of what we were as kingdom people was reserved for the sweet by and by. The part about having been "accepted in the beloved" (Eph. 1:6) and "among whom are ye also the called of Jesus Christ" (Rom. 1:6) didn't filter through.*

That feeling of worthlessness had characterized my whole style of living. And until I could affirm myself as being someone of value, I couldn't really accept others. As the impact of this reality hit me, I began to cry, and my feelings of not being accepted or worthwhile were washed away with those tears. That was probably the first time I really became aware of Danniebelle.

We are all worth something, we are all somebody, and as we become aware of that fact, we begin to see the worth of others. At that point, we can begin to really appreciate them for who they are.

Just Ordinary People
written by Danniebelle Hall

Just ordinary people, God uses ordinary people. He chooses people just like me and you who are willing to do as He commands. God uses people that will give Him all, no matter how small your all may seem to you, because little becomes much as you place it in the Master's hand.

Just ordinary people, my God uses plain old ordinary people (oh yes He does). He chooses people just like me and you who are willing, willing to do everything that He commands. God uses people that will give Him all, no matter how small your all might seem to you, because little becomes much as you place it in the Master's hand.

Just like that little lad who gave Jesus all he had, how the multitude was fed with the fish and the loaves of bread. What you have may not seem much but when you yield it to the touch of the Master's loving hand, yes, then you'll understand how your life could never be the same.

Just ordinary people, my God uses plain old ordinary people (yes). He chooses people just like me and you who are willing to do everything that He commands. God uses people that will give Him all. It doesn't matter, it doesn't matter how small your all may seem to you because little becomes much as you place it in the Master's hand. **(All you've got to do is give your everything to Jesus)**

Little becomes much as you place it in the Master's hand.

Chapter One

Childhood

"Before I formed thee in the belly I knew thee; and before thou camest forth out of the womb I sanctified thee, and I ordained thee a prophet unto the nations." (Jeremiah 1:5)

KEEPING UP WITH THE JONESES

Some families name their offspring after their elders to reinforce the connections between generations. Danniebelle Hall's family observed that custom. Her paternal grandparents were William Bostic Jones and Cynthia Rebecca (Hodges) Jones. In 1890, Cynthia attended Harbison College (Abbeville, SC), and according to family lore, she'd walk for miles, often at night in the dark, to deliver babies. She converted a room of the family home into a schoolroom where she would teach children to read and write. These children could not attend school for several months out of the year because they were required to work on their family's farms.

William and Cynthia had five children. Their eldest, William Butler Jones (b. May 1906), married Danniebell Jones (b. February 1911), who was the only child of Albert Daniel and Seebell Jones (perhaps her name was Sybil, but became "SeeBell" due to southern pronunciation).

Danniebell & William Jones

William Butler and Danniebell met and married at an early age. It was a poignant love story. William, a railroad worker, swept Danniebell, a seamstress, off her feet, to the chagrin of Danniebell's father, who wanted her to attend college. She nicknamed him "Chiddy," and he nicknamed her "Chadeca." They each played various musical instruments, including violin, french horn, piano, and strings. From 1931 to 1951, their East Liberty, Pennsylvania home (on the outskirts of Pittsburgh) was blessed with four boys and four girls. And for the most part, the naming tradition continued.

Danniebell passed her name down to her daughter Danniebelle (adding an "e" at the end), and her younger sister, Cynthia Regelia, inherited her grandmother's name. Later, the name was passed to Danniebelle's daughter, Cynthia Renee.

William and Danniebell's children were William (aka "Bill"), Agnes, Roger, Danniebelle, Henry, Cynthia, Paula, and Sam.

Once Danniebelle had children, she continued the naming tradition. Her children, Charlotte and Charles, are named after their father, Charles Hall.

ALL FARMED OUT

Tragedy struck when the family home burned down in 1954. One day, while Danniebell was at work, Paula saw smoke on the side of the house and ran to get her sister, Cynthia. However, when they returned, the house was engulfed in flames. Reportedly, a pyromaniac living next door was rumored to have burned down nine houses in the neighborhood, including theirs, along with a church. Afterward, the family relocated to Perrysville, Pennsylvania.

Raising eight children wasn't easy, especially after the fire. Financial challenges resulted in six of the eight children, including Danniebelle, being sent to live with various close friends and family members.

Bill, the oldest boy, worked at an orphanage in Florida before joining the Army. Agnes and Cynthia lived with their Uncle Judson and his wife, Dolly, in Butler, Pennsylvania. Roger, who was seven, and Henry, who was just three, moved in with their grandfather, Albert Daniel Jones (Dan), in Mt. Plymouth, Michigan, helping on his hog farm. Paula and Sam were the only two of the eight children that remained in the family home. Danniebelle was just one and was sent to live with family friends Carrie and Clarence Carter (Mama & Papa Carter).

Danniebelle Reflects...

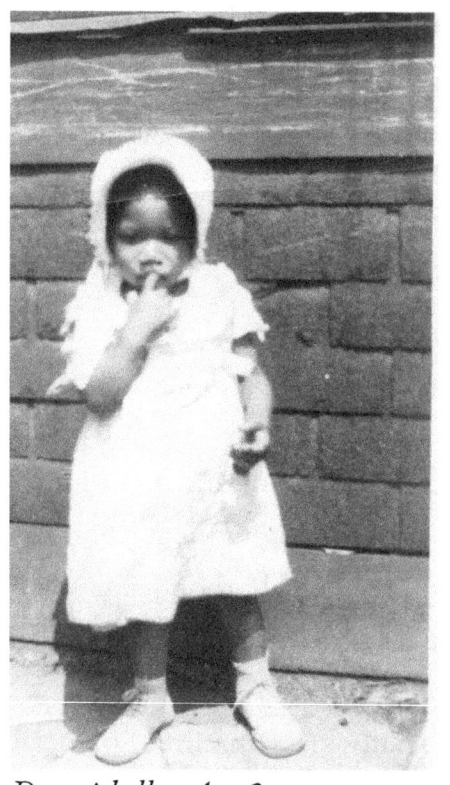

Danniebelle - Age 3

Even though our family [was] large, I didn't know what it was like to grow up close to my brothers and sisters or my Mom and Dad when I was much younger. I was reared in a foster home by friends of the family affectionately known as Mama and Papa Carter.

I'd see my mother in church when she lived near us (in East Liberty), but those church visits diminished when she moved across town. It was a rare treat for me when she'd come and take me to her place in the Perrysville section of Pittsburgh.

All I'd see of my father was when he'd come to the house for his biannual visit. I knew Dad was an easygoing, soft-spoken man who didn't care for arguments. He loved to travel. We'd get together a couple of times a year and take the train to Detroit, where my grandfather lived. Those were the fun times. Getting on the train was always a ritual because we had to pack a huge lunch. My favorite lunch was Mother's potato salad and chipped ham on raisin bread, the kind with the icing and lots of mayonnaise.

Christmas was always a sad time for me because I'd see other kids on the block with toys galore, and all I'd have would be a pair of bedroom slippers. Kids at school used to laugh at the clothes I wore because they were always hand-me-downs that never fit. I could count on getting a new dress or a new pair of shoes two times a year, Easter and my birthday. Seldom was I able to get both at the same time. I was so excited after I grew up and was old enough to take sewing and cooking classes. At least by sewing, I could make clothes that would look better than those old things I'd been wearing.

There were so many months between the times Mom or Dad would visit me. I'd often forget what Mom looked like. There was another lady in our church that I would mistake for her because the two of them looked so much alike to me. Grownups look different through a child's eyes.

MAMA & PAPA CARTER

Carrie and Clarence Carter (Mama & Papa Carter) lived across the backyard from Danniebelle's parents in East Liberty, Pennsylvania, and they all attended East Liberty Church of God. Papa Carter was blind and had a fifth-grade education, and Mama Carter had completed the fourth grade. They didn't have any children of their own.

Danniebelle Reflects...

We lived behind the church, and every Sunday, without fail, some itinerant preacher or some "on fire" missionary would come to our house for dinner. Since I was the only kid there, I often had to wait until the grownups were finished eating, and I was always starved. Mama Carter would always tell visitors, "Help yourself! There's plenty more in the pot."

I'd be thinking, "I wish they'd quit eating so much! I won't have anything left by the time they're finished."

There was this one minister that seemed so strange to me. All of his food had to be specially prepared. He was on a health food kick before it was fashionable. I remember him pulling up his bifocals and checking out the label of the mayonnaise jar, and if the word "egg" appeared in any shape or form, he'd make a big fuss and remind Mama that eggs were bad for you. Mama Carter would smile at him with her inimitable toothless grin and say, "Bro' Ross, what I can't understand about the way you eat is, if eggs is so bad for you, how come you just ate so much of my chicken? They's the ones that makes the eggs in the first place, you know." After dinner would come the heated Bible discussions that could be more accurately described as arguments. By the end of the "discussion," neither side would give. I was always in the middle because Papa Carter was blind, and I had to find the scriptures to support his side of the argument.

Back in those days, the distinction between our church and others was that we were "right," and they weren't. If you didn't belong to THE CHURCH OF GOD, you weren't "truly" saved. In fact, I can recall some of the older saints testifying that they were glad to be saved, sanctified, filled, and belonged to

"C-O-G 14 letters". How shocked I was to discover later that even Presbyterians were Christians.

I remember how genuinely sorry we used to feel for people in those cold, dead, dry churches who had a form of godliness but denied the power of God. The scripture in Rom. 8:11b, which says, "shall also quicken your mortal bodies by his Spirit that dwelleth in you," was taken to mean that if you didn't give a little jerk or shake, then you didn't have the "quickening power" in your life. Even those who were Pentecostal weren't really accepted as part of the body because they didn't carry our brand name. We'd spend so much time poking holes in other folks' doctrines that we never found enough time to accept and love people.

Many organizations are so steeped in tradition that they don't take time to share the message of God's love with the lost without beating them over the head with the gospel whip. And when they aren't scourging the sinner, they turn and find fault with their brothers and sisters because of the differences in the ways they dot their doctrinal I's and cross their theological T's.

What Papa Carter lacked in eyesight, he made up for with his other senses. He'd boast that he could pick up any sound in the house. One day, while Danniebelle and her sister Cynthia were eating and playing together, they decided they would fool Papa Carter. They drank multiple glasses of water until their bellies made gurgling sounds. Then, they tiptoed past him and laid down on the little daybed by the wall, placing their hands on their gurgling stomachs while giggling.

Papa sat at attention in his chair, cocking his head from side to side. "What's that sound?" He demanded, "What did you bring in here?"

"We didn't carry anything in here, Papa Carter! Our hands are empty!" The girls giggled even more as Papa struggled to identify the sound but couldn't.

Papa was humpbacked, and each Sunday, as Danniebelle walked hand in hand with him to church, he'd tap along the sidewalk with his cane. She was always careful and conscientious not to go too fast and to be watchful of the footing along the way. On the other hand, on the few occasions when Paula walked with Papa, she was much less courteous. She'd ask, "Am I walking too fast, Papa Carter?" To which he'd stammer, "No..." through his huffing and puffing. Generally, Paula would abandon Papa once inside the church, and he'd have to tap tap tap his way to the front to find his seat.

One Sunday, Papa and Paula arrived at church after she'd hurriedly led him down the street. Once inside, Danniebelle would sometimes go to Papa to remind him to step down before he proceeded down the aisle to his seat. On this particular Sunday, no one was there to assist, and Papa missed the step down and toppled over to the floor, causing the ushers and others to scramble to help him up and give him the once-over to ensure he was okay. Paula apologized profusely and seemingly learned to be more caring.

While living with the Carters, Danniebelle began taking piano lessons. Although she loved the piano, practicing often took second place to roller skating with her best friend, Penny. As a compromise, Danniebelle would often practice her lessons with her roller skates on.

Danniebelle Reflects...

People often asked me, "How long have you been playing the piano?" As far back as I can remember – nursery school, kindergarten – I was playing "My Country 'Tis of Thee." I took piano lessons from the time I was six 'til I was

CHILDHOOD   9

twelve. My teacher, George, was a phenomenal jazz pianist – turned preacher. He was an unusual person. He only taught people that he felt were worth his time. If he came to your house and listened to you and didn't feel you had the potential to become an artist, he'd tell you at the outset, "I can't teach you." I guess George had a certain feel for who could and who couldn't. And if he thought you couldn't, he just wouldn't bother to show up for the next lesson.

He'd come to the house sometimes once a week, sometimes every two weeks, or maybe only once a month, but eventually, he would show up. He had a way of conveying whole concepts as well as specific executions. For instance, he knew I'd eventually want to play in the church, so he taught me basic patterns of most of the songs we sang in our church, and when I'd play for services (I was probably around 10 or 11 when I started playing for service), I'd apply the basic chord patterns to whatever key the song was in.

Church was where I learned to improvise and develop my own style. I started playing at services when I was 13. I can remember going with the choir, congregation, and pastor to various fellowship meetings. Service would usually begin with us singing from the hymn books, and then we'd put the books down and "have church!" When we put the books down, someone might decide to start a song in B flat, and I had to find that key. A few months of that kind of playing, and you automatically develop

Young Danniebelle

relative pitch. I was always glad when Sister Harvey started a song because her pitch was so flexible; you could persuade her to sing in the nearest easy key just *by playing the dominant note of the desired key really loud. She'd slide up to it every time!*

My whole world was playing for the choir.

I wasn't intimidated, but I would never sing. Nobody asked me to sing, so there was no need to even try. At some point, my older sister, Agnes, had the bright idea of the two of us traveling around to various church teas as "The Jones Duo." I just sort of tagged along.

One time, Mom, Agnes, and I went to sing at a social function at someone's house. As the evening progressed, it was obvious that it wasn't the kind of gathering we were accustomed to. My mom quickly rose up in righteous indignation and informed those gathered that she and her girls felt like fish out of water and would have no part in a social of "this" nature. Actually, we were intrigued by the whole thing and would have stayed longer if Mom hadn't spoken up.

That was my first taste of life outside the church world. I lived a very sheltered life and was quite content not knowing what 'the world' was like. In reflection, I probably was too afraid to investigate the things that the devil had to offer. I had heard so many testimonies of how God had delivered others from a miserable life of sin and how 'there was nothing out there.' But what I couldn't figure out was, if "the world" was as bad as people said, why were there so many folks out there in it? For a long time, I didn't realize the blindness that Satan causes to come over people, and I had no compassion for people that were bound by habits and lifestyles. It wasn't until after I moved away from that sheltered environment that I began to see what really happens to people that are fooled into thinking they're having a good time.

I decided at one point in my life that I was going to "live it up." I'd sneak off to nightclubs and order drinks. I didn't even know what to order. I'd sit and listen to the music and watch folks dance. I had always wanted to dance, but every time the kids on the block would try to teach me, they'd give up on me, saying something like 'I had two left feet' or 'I danced like their grandma.' The only dancing I could do was square dancing, but there just didn't seem to be much of a demand for promenades and Dosey Doe's in the nightclubs. So I'd just sit and watch. The lewd little sip of my drink would make me dizzy, and the band was always playing too loudly for conversation with other people. In simple words, I was miserable. So were many of the other people that were there. They just didn't have anywhere else to go.

Danniebelle lived with Mama and Papa Carter until she was fifteen. She graduated from Peabody High School a year later and moved back home with her parents in Perrysville, Pennsylvania. She began attending Mount Mercy Catholic College on a scholarship and majored in Home Economics before moving to California.

Chapter Two

Early Family Life

"Train up a child in the way he should go: and when he is old, he will not depart from it." (Proverbs 22:6)

CALIFORNIA – HERE I COME!

Danniebelle Reflects...

As I grew older, I realized that I was the only one in my family who hadn't made the trip to California with Daddy. Once a year, the Pennsylvania Railroad Company would issue him an inter-company travel pass. Chicago was as far as the pass would allow him to go, but Daddy loved California, especially the weather.

In 1958, I went to California with Daddy. I only brought two suits and a couple skirts and blouses. I expected to stay two weeks, but the Lord had other plans. After two weeks in Los Angeles, Mrs. Anna McKnight, a friend and the sister of my pastor's wife in Pittsburgh, asked me if I'd like to come to San Francisco and live with her and her husband. He pastored a church there and needed a pianist. It sounded all right to me because, at the time, I couldn't think of anything better to do. I had just dropped out of college after two-and-a-half years.

Mrs. McKnight, who we affectionately called Mother, and her husband, Elder McKnight, or Daddy Tim, always fascinated me. She was always beautifully dressed and had classy jewelry and furs. I figured that all Californians dressed like that. He was a huge man, dressed immaculately, wore several rings on his fingers, and always carried a fan in his hand. To me, he was the epitome of success.

After arriving in San Francisco, I began to see how God was piecing my "life puzzle" together. I recall praying one afternoon while I was in the bathroom. The Lord indelibly impressed in my mind, "Stay in California and preach my word."

My immediate response was, "Lord, is this really you?"
His reply was, "When I tell you something, don't question it."
"Yes Lord," I responded, "Whatever you want is what I want."

Since I was a child, I recall experiencing the voice of the Lord. Sometimes He'd speak to me through books. At the age of 10, I read John Milton's "Paradise Lost" and John Bunyan's "The Pilgrim's Progress," I was moved to tears as I perceived the struggles that God's children face. I was overwhelmed by the temptations and conflicts that I knew I'd have to face, but I also became aware of a presence and a power that had already overcome the enemy of my soul if I would only stop and listen to God's guidance.

Children have the capacity to comprehend so much more than grownups give them credit for, and their minds are not nearly as cluttered with mundane distractions. They have an incredible way of seeing simple truths that often elude adults. It's important to give children the proper tools early in life so that they can build on a firm foundation. Children should be encouraged to be an active part in family devotions and be taught to pray aloud. So often, we think they're going to make a mistake or not say things right. Have you ever really listened to a child pray? Their prayers are simple and direct. Without beating around the bush or sugar-coating, they go right to the core of the matter.

TO HAVE AND TO HOLD

Lighthouse Full Gospel was a very small church, more like a family. Elder and Mrs. McKnight became Danniebelle's parents, and Mrs. McKnight's sister and brother-in-law, Retha and Cornelius, were her newfound siblings. Retha treated Danniebelle with sisterly love and generosity — something she wasn't accustomed to.

Danniebelle Reflects...

It takes a greater amount of grace to receive love than it does to give it. Although it's more blessed to give, there is an art to receiving. It goes back to a very basic idea of being able to accept ourselves as we are. Real meekness carries that kind of knowledge with it – knowing your worth as well as your limitations and being able to accept and operate within those parameters. Receiving love from those dear people reshaped my life.

Retha worked at one of the hospitals in San Francisco, California. One day, she told me about a really nice guy that she worked with. She wanted to know if it was all right to give him my phone number. The first thing I asked was, "Is he saved?" That was considered standard information in my church. If he wasn't saved, you just didn't talk to him. Well, he wasn't, but she said he was a good person and would probably get saved right away.

I marvel at how we find it difficult to accept people as they are. As it turned out, Charles Hall had a lot more virtues, higher standards, and moral ethics than some of my Christian friends.

The first time he called, we talked for two hours, trying to learn what it was that we might have in common so we could justify building a relationship. He immediately wanted to know what I looked like. I figured I didn't have too much going for me when there was a two-minute pause on my end. "Well," I said, "I never thought that looks were that important. It's the personality that really counts, and I think I have a pleasant personality. "What about you? What do you look like?" There wasn't a moment's hesitation on his part. "I'm tall, dark, and handsome with curly hair." This I had to see for myself. The minute I met him, I knew he was Mr. Right. He later confessed to me that it was my legs and the view from the rear as I walked up the stairs in front of him that was the start of what blossomed into a mad love affair.

Danniebelle & Charles Hall

Charles was impressed with the fact that the only thing I ever did was go to church and that I seemed happy about it. He became inquisitive, and I simply shared Jesus Christ with him. Within three weeks, he accepted Christ, and six months later, we were married. He was the last new convert at Lighthouse before Elder McKnight's untimely death. Daddy Tim led Charles to the Lord from Rom. 10:9-10, "if thou shalt confess with thy mouth the Lord Jesus, and shalt believe in thine heart that God hath raised him from the dead, thou shalt be saved. For with the heart man believeth unto righteousness; and with the mouth confession is made unto salvation."

If I had refused Charles' friendship on the basis that he wasn't a professing Christian, we may never have gotten to know each other well enough to want to join our lives together, and we wouldn't have been blessed with three beautiful children.

There were times that we wondered if we were going to be able to hang together. Usually, at the base of our problems was the fact that we failed to take advantage of the privilege of prayer. As we prayed together and as we would hear each other verbalize our needs, we would sense the power of the Holy Spirit welding us together. As Charles would ask God to supply a need within me, there would rise the desire to be all that I could be to him, to just be there to comfort and affirm him and let him know that I believed in him. Sometimes we don't realize what our mate needs until we hear them asking God for it. That's part of the joy of praying together.

Before we said, "I do," Charles got laid off from his job. But since we had already made plans for the ceremony, we decided against postponing it. We were so very much in love and wanted to be together. So, we were willing to enter into marriage without being financially secure. I had confidence in Charles' ambition but more than that, I trusted the Lord's ability to help him find a job. After a month of searching, he found a job that didn't pay very much but met our needs. I had an income, so we were able to budget and manage to make ends meet. It was a frugal beginning, but we had each other.

OUR GROWING FAMILY

A year and a half into our marriage, I got pregnant. We knew that the baby would put a big dent in our budget since I wouldn't be able to work after the baby came. Fortunately, because I worked for the Federal Government, I was able to join a group health plan that provided excellent prenatal care. I felt overwhelmed by the thought of having to care for a baby. After all, I'd never had much experience with babies. A while back, when my older sister let me change a baby's diaper, I couldn't seem to coordinate my movements with the baby's. We both agreed I probably wasn't quite ready to be a mom. I wanted my Mom with me, but along with Mom came my youngest sister, Paula, and baby brother, Sam.

Before we were married, I had already sent for my sister Cynthia. All this added more strain to our budget. To accommodate all those people, we moved out of our flat into a three-bedroom home that we rented from my mother-in-law.

I'll never forget how Charles would come home from work every day and find me sitting in the middle of the floor sucking ice cubes because the doctor didn't want me drinking too much water. My feet and hands swelled so badly. Each evening without fail, he'd ask me, "You haven't had my baby yet?" Finally, one morning at about 4 am, a few signs indicated that the fullness of time had come. Eight hours and many pains later, I heard our little girl Charlotte Elaine cry. What a beautiful sound!

GROWING PAINS

Our small home and budget were soon challenged to the breaking point. One of my older brothers and his new bride also moved in, making for eight mouths to feed, and Charles was the only one working. The strain was too much. We started getting on each other's nerves and yelling and screaming at each other for no apparent reason.

Finally, I exploded and ordered everybody out of the house. Soon, Charles, the baby, and I were the only ones living there.

Shortly after that, I became pregnant again. This time, my father came out to help take care of me. Little did I know this would be the last time I'd see him alive. Months later, Charles Timothy was born. What a whopper he was, 9 lbs 3 oz! A year and a half later, Cynthia Renee was born.

The Halls

Daddy died before I got a chance to really know him, but from what I learned about him, there are similarities in our personalities. I inherited his love for languages and people. He was a gourmet chef and had quite a sense of humor. He enjoyed making people happy and would go to great lengths to do so.

I worried about whether Daddy would make it to heaven. He died in a hospital in Cleveland, Ohio, before any of us knew how sick he was. Some people said slanderous things about him. But one night after his death, I dreamt that Daddy was standing in front of the church leading the song service. He stopped and asked my brother Henry and me to come and play for him. Then he said, "While my children are coming up here, I just want to say that a lot of you have been talking about Bro. Jones doing things he shouldn't do...and some of you are right, but I want to know who of us in here has never done things he shouldn't do? God has forgiven me for everything I've done, and I'm going home to be with Jesus."

Since then, I've never worried about my father.

So often, when you're reared in a legalistic sheltered environment, as I was, you never realize what people outside of your environment are searching for. You're only told that these things are bad for you, but you never know why. I've come to realize that there is a void in everyone's life that needs to be filled by the Spirit of God. But unless we recognize that we need God's Spirit, we can spend an entire lifetime trying to fill that void with whatever brings satisfaction, things like drugs and sex. What many people don't realize is that these are only temporary stop-gap measures.

As we've sung "It Won't Be Long" by Andraé Crouch, a tear sometimes trickles down my cheek because it incorporates one of Daddy's favorite scriptures. 1 Thess. 4:15-16 says, "For this we say unto you by the word of the Lord, that we which are alive and remain unto the coming of the Lord shall not prevent them which are asleep. For the Lord himself shall descend from heaven with a shout, with the voice of the archangel, and with the trump of God: and the dead in Christ shall rise first."

Daddy explained that the word "prevent" in the 15th verse had nothing to do with our present-day connotation of "a hindrance" or "trying to stop something." Instead, it meant that those who are alive won't precede those who are asleep in Jesus. One thing I look forward to in heaven is knowing my Daddy and being able to share, along with him, the pure love of Christ throughout eternity. That's a hope that nothing in this world can wrestle away from me.

It won't be long.

Chapter Three

The Danniebelles

"Make a joyful noise unto the Lord, all the earth: make a loud noise, and rejoice, and sing praise." (Psalm 98:4)

DO YOU HAVE A GROUP?

Danniebelle Reflects...

The first time I remember singing before a large audience was at one of Audrey Meirs' Sing-A-Longs in 1969. Audrey's heart was as big as the world's. She had a way of becoming your Mama before you knew it, and she always seemed to get the biggest thrill out of introducing new talent. When I sang "Great Is Thy Faithfulness," I thought she would go into orbit. She laid hands on me and had the audience stretch their hands toward me. I thought she was carrying it just a little too far when she prophesied very forthrightly and unhesitantly about my ministry, predicting that I would share Christ in a way that would touch the lives of thousands of people.

Shortly after that, a gentleman approached Danniebelle and asked if she'd be interested in recording.

"Do you have a group?" he asked.
"No," she answered.
"Can you get a group?"
"Yes!"

Initially, the group consisted of Danniebelle, Jimmye Jackson, Phyllis Swisher, and Brenda Williams. Later, Danniebelle's sister, Paula joined, and Brenda's sisters, Barbara and Janice Williams joined as alternates. As they were preparing for their first recording, *Make The Most of Today*, the gentleman asked, "What do you call yourselves?" They settled on the name,

The Danniebelles. "Belles" was drawn from Danniebelle's name and Psalm 98, where David writes: "make a joyful noise unto the Lord."

The Danniebelles

In December 1969, at a small recording studio in San Francisco, The Danniebelles recorded their debut album. The group became known for wearing beautiful African dashiki-style dresses complemented by glorious 1970s Afros. Danniebelle accompanied the group on piano and arranged the tight vocal harmonies. She wrote the title song while group member Phyllis Swisher wrote and sang the beautiful song "The Rain Is Falling." The album cover featured a collage of photos taken during the studio session and a festival appearance at the Sweet Jesus Roll Away the Stone held at Stanford University.

THE JESUS MOVEMENT

The Danniebelles were a massive part of what became known as "The Jesus Movement," an evangelical Christian movement during the late 60s and early 70s. They would minister at various events and meet other young people who wanted to involve themselves in the Movement.

Danniebelle Reflects...

The Danniebelles held small group meetings very similar to the Faith At Work meetings. Through these settings, we would come into contact and work with such groups as Young Life, Youth For Christ, Intervarsity Campus Crusade, and others. We would go to the point of exhaustion, but we were so overjoyed at what we were seeing – people turning their lives over to Jesus.

Sometimes, after a meeting, we'd go back to our home church and share what the Lord was doing. A few folks would express how glad they were for our involvement, but there were others that were indifferent or hostile. They felt that we were "out in left field" because we weren't at church all the time. It was strange to me that I could go out and be received and accepted by strangers, but at home, folks were putting me down. I cried night after night and began to question the Lord. "Am I out of Your will? Is this the way it should be?"

WORLD VISION TOUR – SOUTHEAST ASIA

The Danniebelles became extremely popular and traveled to engagements practically every weekend, frequently rehearsing in Danniebelle's garage.

Danniebelle Reflects...

One night, in the middle of a Mount Hermon Christian Conference Center concert, I shared that our greatest desire was to travel overseas and spread the good news. After the concert, an extremely tall man walked up to me. I'm only 5'2," so nearly everyone over 6' seems extra tall. I kept looking up, and up until finally, our eyes met. "So you'd like to travel, would you?" I nodded. I hadn't quite come down from my "Holy Spirit high," but I was trying to relate to what my ears were hearing.

This tall, distinguished man with a deeply furrowed brow and eyes that seemed to anticipate anything I'd say told me that he'd like to make our dreams come true. He was Ted Engstrom, Vice President of World Vision.

He wanted The Danniebelles to participate in crusades in the Philippines and Cambodia with Dr. Stan Mooneyham. It sounded great, but I wasn't sure he was serious. That conversation took place in the summer of 1971. A few months went by, and we were invited to a banquet sponsored by World Vision. That's when I began to understand the magnitude of work involved in a crusade of this nature. This wasn't just another series of concerts. We were about to be involved in a global move of the Holy Spirit.

The banquet was a tremendous success. People were made aware of the needs in Vietnam and Cambodia, and they generously responded. We became preoccupied with getting visas and passports ready for what would prove to be one of the Danniebelles' most exciting experiences.

Off we flew to Southeast Asia. We were scheduled to meet Dr. Mooneyham and the crusade team in Manila, but we had a few stopovers on the way.

Our first stop was in Hawaii, where a couple of engagements had been pre-arranged with Bob Turnbull's huge ministry. The service was held right on Waikiki Beach. It was my first time seeing people come to church in bathing suits. What an experience!

After leaving Hawaii, we went to Tokyo. We all had decided that we were going straight to the hotel and to bed. The Okura hotel (The Pearl of the Orient) was grand and impressive, but we were exhausted. We got our keys and headed toward our rooms, but all of a sudden, we looked across the lobby and saw Muhammad Ali in all of his splendor and glory. He spied us at the same time and opened his arms wide enough to engulf all four of us and yelled, "Sisters!" We completely forgot all of our weariness; I think we even forgot where we were. We dropped everything and rushed into those big strong arms.

Ali was in Japan to train for his fight with Mack Foster. He had an entourage of at least 15 to 20 people, including his Mom, who said she'd seen us on one of Billy Graham's telecasts.

I said to him, "Look, I'm a married woman, got a husband and three kids, and I'm not trying to run a game, but would you just let me touch your arm? Please, sir?" He laughed, showing all of those beautiful teeth, and said, "I ain't nothing but a plain old niggah!" to which I replied (with levity), "Yes, but you are such a FINE niggah!"

We must have talked half the night away. He kept coming out with those limericks for which he's so famous. We finally decided it was time to go to sleep, but I couldn't really sleep; I was just trying to get over the shock of seeing Muhammad Ali.

The next day, on our way to the Philippines, we decided to take pictures with Ali and get his autograph. Jimmye asked him to sign for one of her cousins, who was a boxer. Ali asked, "and what does he box apples or oranges?" His joking and quick wit was hilarious.

THE CRUSADES

After a few days and appearances in Manila, we flew to the island of Mindanao, at the southeastern tip of the Philippine Islands. The crusades there were held in the remote town of Zamboanga, in a large open field. Each night, thousands would attend. Many had never experienced a crusade or seen Black people. They were wild about the Danniebelles and knew all of our names – Danniebelle Hall, Phyllis Swisher, Paula Jones, and Jimmye Jackson. They'd often ask Jimmye, "You Five Jackson?" She'd laugh and respond, "No. Just one Jackson."

The Philippine Crusades were historic. They took place in the mid-70s shortly before the fall of Cambodia and Phnom Penh and marked the beginning of the Khmer Rouge takeover. These were the first public evangelistic meetings ever held in Cambodia.

After Cambodia, The Danniebelles traveled to Southeast Asia, this time with the USO. They spent two weeks in Vietnam and another two in Thailand. Their mission to share the good news of Jesus Christ wasn't easy, and they often dealt with spiritual warfare, but they loved the Lord and worked hard at their assignment. One comical aspect was the bugs in the region. While performing, the ladies had a deal. If a bug landed on someone, the lady standing beside that person would brush it off and keep singing.

Danniebelle Reflects...

If you ever decide you want to write a situation comedy, form a singing group of Black women, and travel with them. You'll have enough material to fill volumes.

Most of the concerts in the Philippines were in high schools and colleges, but one was in a leper colony. We were advised that there was nothing to be afraid of because the disease was not contagious, but we were not to make physical contact with anyone who had running or open sores. There was a distinct odor about the camp. I must admit to a minimal amount of apprehension coupled with just a twinge of fear of what we would encounter.

As I stood singing, suddenly, I sensed the compassion of Jesus, the likes of which I had never experienced before nor since. I was standing that day where Christ would have stood when He was here physically on earth. We were singing, but it wasn't really us; it was like Jesus was singing to these people and using our voices. The feeling was so intense and overwhelming that as the people began to sing along with us, "Yes, Jesus Loves Me," the tears flowed from our eyes like an unending river.

We were actually touching people's lives in Jesus' stead. I felt what Jesus must have felt when He saw those ten lepers bound by that dreadful disease that cut them off from society. He spoke words of healing, and they were cleansed. All I could do was stand there and cry and feel. Time after time, I was moved to tears by the things I experienced on that tour.

From 1969 to 1972, The Danniebelles ministered at various crusades and festivals, including Billy Graham crusades. In 1972, they traveled to Jamaica with Ralph Bell, an associate evangelist with Billy Graham. This was one of their last appearances as The Danniebelles before Danniebelle began singing with Andrae Crouch and The Disciples. The ladies remained friends.

Chapter Four

Andrae Crouch & The Disciples

"And he said unto them, Go ye into all the world, and preach the gospel to every creature." (Mark 16:15)

BECOMING A DISCIPLE

Andrae Crouch & the Disciples became widely acknowledged as one of the top groups in Christian music ministry between the mid-60s to the late 70s. As a group, The Disciples originated with Andrae, his twin sister Sandra, Bili Thedford, Sherman Andrus, Ruben Fernandez, and Perry Morgan.

In 1969, when The Danniebelles recorded the album, *Making The Most of Today,* they included "I Didn't Think It Could Be," a song written by Andrae. Perhaps by coincidence or providence, the two groups were invited to appear in the Bay Area on the same program. Andrae was impressed with The Danniebelles' sound, and in 1973 after Sherman Andrus left the Disciples to join The Imperials, he invited Danniebelle to join. She accepted.

The Disciples traveled nationally and internationally and included musical giants such as Bill Maxwell (drums), Harlan Rogers (guitar), Fletch Wiley (horns), and Hadley Hockensmith (keyboards). All were former members of the Christian group, Sonlight. Additional members, Bea Carr, James Felix, Jimmie Davis, and Mike Escalante joined the group in the following years.

In 1975, The Disciples won the Grammy Award for Best Soul Gospel Performance for *Take Me Back,* and in 1978 they won Best Contemporary Soul Gospel Album for *Live in London.* Twenty years later, in 1998, Andrae was inducted into the Gospel Music Association's Hall of Fame.

LIFE ON THE ROAD

The Disciples obtained their tour bus, affectionately dubbed "Ruby," from Buck and Dottie Rambo. As they traveled throughout cities and states across the U.S., group member Perry Morgan became the designated driver.

Danniebelle's first tour with The Disciples began in 1973 on the heels of the release of *Live at Carnegie Hall* which became one of The Disciples' landmark albums.

Danniebelle Reflects...

I saw Andrae literally pour himself out to audiences night after night. And afterward, despite being drained, clothes soaked, and hungry, he would stop and talk with various individuals.

Immediately following a concert, most Christian artists experience a wide range of emotions. First, there's the emotional high from being used by God to bless His people. Then, you feel gratified to hear the applause and comments like "You really blessed me tonight" or "What you said tonight sure helped me." Finally, and most difficult, is the time after the applause and thank you's end. Whether you are a solo artist or part of a group, Satan uses that time to make you feel desperately alone.

I quickly learned not to hoard any of the adulation and praise from the crowd for myself but to give all the glory back to God. When people would tell me how much my ministry meant to them, I would only accept the praise for a job well done because I knew that the glory belonged to God, and He wouldn't share His glory with anyone.

Reportedly, Janis Joplin made note of the stark contrast between a stadium filled with roaring fans and the deafening silence once the stadium emptied. "Where are they now?" she would ask. One moment, everyone loves you, and the next, you slip into anonymity. Those silent moments have driven many entertainers, including many in the Christian/gospel music field, to the edge. They constantly seek to fill the void of loneliness with anything that's available. The question is, "Can you resist the temptation of a lifestyle that is contrary to everything you just shared with the crowd a few minutes ago?"

Performers are most vulnerable to a satanic attack after the concert, although it would seem that just the opposite would be true. After sharing the good news of Jesus, you should be on cloud nine or in the seventh heaven. The secret is to recognize Satan's tactics, and when you sense yourself being drawn into that web, claim the Father's strength. His grace is sufficient for you. He is with you, and He's all you need. His power shows up in times when you are weak. (see 2 Cor. 12:9) Praise the Lord for another chance to be a showcase for His grace.

Another helpful hint is to keep your mind occupied with something stimulating, challenging, and worthwhile. Then, you will be less likely to succumb to bouts of loneliness. The best focus of meditation is God's Word.

Usually, right after a concert, I find myself so high that it takes me a long time to wind down. There's so much energy that goes into singing and sharing. Afterward, the tendency is to want to "let your hair down," as if we feel accountable to the Lord only for what we do on stage, and afterward, our time is our own. In reality, our time is not our own if we have, in fact, given ourselves completely to the Lord. Our time and what we do with that important commodity belong to Him.

In addition to a lot of singing and prayer, the Disciples also shared a lot of laughter and good food while traveling together. They often traveled during the holidays. One year, during Thanksgiving, the group was in Florida, and actress Diahann Carroll invited them to her home for Thanksgiving dinner. Danniebelle was known for finding the best places to eat. She'd say, "I got the bag. I got the bag!"

In New York, just as the group finished a concert at Carnegie Hall before a sold-out crowd, Danniebelle headed to Juniors Restaurant and Bakery for a huge slice of strawberry cheesecake. Although she would try to watch her weight while on the road, the good food was too much to resist. She'd order a slice of cheesecake along with a diet Coke. Once, in Detroit, "Mom" Winans (mother of the gospel family, The Winans) brought sweet potato pies for the group. Often, the group would have food waiting for them following a concert. She always missed her family. So, whenever she got a chance, she'd call home. She'd say, "I gotta call my babies! I gotta call my babies!"

A VESSEL THROUGH WHICH HIS LOVE CAN FLOW

Danniebelle was in her mid-30s by the time she joined The Disciples. Most of the group members, including Andrae, were younger than her, so she took on a "mother hen" role. She would sense when a group member was going through something. She'd say, "Hey, is everything alright? Do you need to talk? Let's take a walk." Danniebelle always had time to listen, pray, or console anyone who was hurting. She was a great example of Christian love and compassion.

One time following a concert, Andrae had an altar call. Reba Rambo, daughter of Dottie Rambo, was on the stage singing with the group. Danniebelle grabbed Reba's hand and went down the steps into the audience, where people were receiving prayer. There was a young girl around 13 or 14, crying and sobbing. Danniebelle hugged her and began to pray for her. She began to talk to the young girl and said, "A little birdie told me...." This was one of Danniebelle's ways of approaching someone with a word from God. "The Holy Ghost dove" would use her prophetically to speak into other people's lives.

Andrae often asked Danniebelle to sing before the group went on stage. Her singing would create such an atmosphere of spiritual intimacy with the Lord that when she finished, people were ready to worship. As she ministered through song or shared her testimony, people felt as though she was speaking directly to their personal circumstances.

Danniebelle loved old hymns, and she interpreted them with a freshness and depth of feeling. Her singing made the hymns come alive, not like recitations out of a book. Musically, she wore her heart on her sleeve. More than just a singer, she ministered powerfully through music and changed lives. As she played the piano, the Holy Spirit would come in. At times, she'd wait and just play and not sing. She gave the audience a playbook on how to praise and worship God.

GOING SOLO

As part of The Disciples, Danniebelle participated on recordings: *Take Me Back (1975), This Is Another Day (1976),* and *Live in London (1978).* Her voice and style were unique and immediately identifiable. She ministered on several songs including, "Take Me Back," "Soon & Very Soon," "Tell Them," and "My Peace I Leave With You."

Apart from The Disciples, Danniebelle began to receive invitations to sing and minister. Sometimes, one of the band members would accompany her, but most of the time, she'd go by herself. Although she was a hymnist, her vocal and keyboard performance style was not traditional gospel.

People compared her to Roberta Flack. She was one of the pioneers of 1970s contemporary Christian music and one of the few Black female contemporary gospel solo artists.

Launching out as a solo artist, Danniebelle recorded several albums, including *Danniebelle (1974)*, *This Moment (1975)*, *He Is King (1976)*, *Let Me Have A Dream (1977)*, and *Danniebelle Live in Sweden with Choralerna (1978)*. In 1977, she received a Grammy nomination for Best Contemporary Soul Gospel Album for *He Is King*, and a year later, another Grammy nod for *Danniebelle Live in Sweden with Choralerna*.

The Disciples' drummer, Bill Maxwell, produced each of Danniebelle's albums during that period. After working with Andrae on an album by gospel group Sweet Spirit, which included Disciples group members Bea Carr and Kathy Hazzard, Bill started producing. They were the first group to record "Take Me Back."

Each of Danniebelle's albums would include a traditional hymn. Of course, Danniebelle would add her own unique arrangement to it. She'd say, "I think it should be this way, Bill."

He'd respond, "You're the singer and the artist, but I'm the painter. I will put it on the canvas."

They had a wonderful friendship.

In 1978, Danniebelle traveled to Chicago to be a part of Rev. Jesse Jackson's recording, *Push For Excellence*. The following year, the album was nominated for Best Contemporary Soul Gospel Album.

On *Danniebelle Live in Sweden*, Danniebelle arranged and recorded Dottie Rambo's composition, "I Go To The Rock." However, when Whitney Houston recorded the song for the soundtrack of the movie, *The Preacher's Wife*, Danniebelle's arrangement was used.

Chapter Five

On Her Own

"And we know that all things work together for good to them that love God, to them who are the called according to his purpose." (Romans 8:28)

LITTLE BECOMES MUCH

In 1977, Danniebelle recorded the hallmark album, *Let Me Have a Dream,* which contained the signature song "Ordinary People." It became one of her most famous compositions.

Danniebelle was known to wake up early in the morning to play or pen a song God had placed in her heart. She'd go into the living room, sit at her baby grand piano, hum the tune, play a few chords, and write words on a notepad that she kept close by. It was the same process for "Ordinary People," however, when she finished it and played it for her husband, he said, "Danniebelle! You've outdone yourself with this one!"

In John 6:9-11, Jesus asked a young boy to share his two fish and five loaves of bread with a huge crowd of people. Jesus' disciples marveled at the outlandish request but even more at the miracle which followed, as thousands were fed from such a small offering. This Bible story was the basis of "Ordinary People." The song spread like wildfire. It became a signature song for the beautiful, rich, deep, bass-baritone voice of singer/songwriter Wintley Phipps.

In 1984, when Rev. Jesse Jackson invited Wintley to sing at the Democratic National Convention, they both agreed that "Ordinary People" was the perfect song to precede Rev. Jackson's keynote speech. Unfortunately, there were so many speakers that preceded Rev. Jackson that the producers cut the song from the program.

Rev. Jackson's speech electrified the convention. The crowd cheered and clapped for several minutes. While they were applauding, Rev. Jackson walked over to Wintley and said, "You got the music? Go up there and hit it!" Millions of viewers heard Wintley sing "Ordinary People." It was an extraordinary moment.

Danniebelle sat in her bedroom that night watching her television with tears streaming down her face thinking, *"He's singing my song!"* The moment was unforgettable!

LIFE AT HOME

Charles and Danniebelle Hall were married for fifteen years when she joined The Disciples. She was 35, and their children were 13, 11, and 8. As their financial situation improved, the Halls moved from their tiny two-bedroom home in E. Palo Alto to a larger home in San Jose and then to an even larger home in the Alum Rock Hills area of San Jose. They called it "The big house on the hill."

Charles fully supported Danniebelle's ministry and calling. When it became apparent that she'd be traveling a lot, they both sat down with their children to explain why their mother would be leaving periodically and what she'd be doing. When they asked the children to share their feelings, they expressed that they missed their mom when she was gone and loved it when she'd come back home.

When possible, during the summer months, while the children were out of school, the entire family would travel to various engagements. Charles didn't care much for travel, but he did accompany Danniebelle to Australia and a few other select dates.

The Halls were known to open their home to many people. Some left lasting memories, while others caused damage beyond repair.

Shelley Lott was a woman from Texas with a generous heart and a caring spirit who brought nothing but joy and laughter into the Hall home. When

Andrae and The Disciples would perform near Houston, Shelley would often prepare food and take it to the hotel for them to enjoy after the concert. On one such occasion, Danniebelle told her that anytime she came to California, she could stay with the Hall family. Shelley took her up on the offer. She came for a visit and ended up staying five or six years and helped with the household and children while Danniebelle was on the road. Shelley was a blessing and became part of the Hall family.

When Danniebelle's son Charles was fifteen, he stayed with Andrae at his house for a couple of months during the summer. One afternoon, while Andrae was napping, Charles decided to take Andrae's car out for a spin around the block. He'd gotten away with it before, and as mischievous teens often do, he decided to try it again. This time he drove a bit further. While stopped at a red light in a busy intersection, a cop drove up in the next lane. When the light turned green, Charles froze. The cop nudged him with his eyes to drive forward, and when he didn't, the cop pulled him over.

The police drew their guns and told Charles to put his hands up. Charles was petrified. Here was a young black kid in Los Angeles driving a Mercedes Benz. He tried to explain that it was his uncle's car, but they called Andrae, who had to come to get Charles and the car.

Andrae said nothing except, "You know I'm gonna have to get you when we get back to the house." When they got back, Andrae talked to Charles about right and wrong. He said, "I understand why a kid would do that, but you understand, it's wrong. So, I am going to have to chastise you." He then spanked Charles, and that was the end of it. Andrae told Charles to think about what he'd done, and they didn't talk about it anymore.

Looking back, Charles can appreciate the many "valleys" and unfavorable circumstances he experienced as a teen. They allowed him to see God's hand in his life, drawing him closer to what God has purposed for Charles to be and do.

Life at home for the Hall family was as every day as possible. When Danniebelle was home, she loved to spend time with her family and watch shows like "Good Times" and "Sanford and Son." Charles Sr. loved the show and laughed at Redd Foxx's antics.

The Hall Family

The family would play games together like spades, checkers, monopoly, and rummy. Danniebelle and her son Charles would sit and play rummy for hours. She was highly competitive and played with determination and tenacity.

Their favorite game was Othello, a combination of checkers and chess. When Charles would think about his next play, Dannibelle would interrupt his concentration and ask, "Are you sure that's what you want to do, son? Be careful before you make your next move because it could come back to bite you! I don't know if you want to do that."

Once Charles made his move, he couldn't take it back. It was a game, but she was also teaching her son to think about making moves, taking risks, and considering repercussions in life.

Danniebelle was a local celebrity in the San Francisco Bay Area. In the spirit of Audrey Meier's Sing-A-Long shows, Danniebelle hosted a television show on local channel 42 out of Concord, California, featuring local talent and guests called "Sing-A-Long with Danniebelle."

When Andrae Crouch and The Disciples would come to town, they'd park "Ruby" right on the street in front of Danniebelle's home. Neighbors didn't complain; in fact, they would move their cars to make way for the huge bus.

Danniebelle loved to cook and would prepare delicious meals for her family and friends. When The Winans released their album, *Introducing The Winans,* brothers Marvin, Carvin, Ronald, and Michael, along with Vickie Winans (Marvin's wife), visited Danniebelle's home. They made themselves at home, sang tunes around the piano, and laughed. At a point, the brothers joined together to rework the Burger King jingle singing, "Aren't you hungry, aren't you hungry? Aren't you hungry for Jesus Christ now!"

THE ULTIMATE SACRIFICE

For Danniebelle, leaving her family for long periods of time to travel around the world was not something done on a whim. It was organic to her ministry and grew as Danniebelle followed her life's calling. At first, when The Danniebelles began traveling, Danniebelle's entire family would accompany the group to their local engagements; however, things changed following the *Live at Carnegie Hall* recording with The Disciples.

Danniebelle Reflects...

I've experienced a great deal of criticism from many well-meaning and honestly concerned brothers and sisters to the tune of, "You have no business leaving your husband and your family like that. You should be at home," or "You should only travel with your family. You're neglecting your obligation as a wife and mother."

This would all be accurate if it were not for a truth that I have clung to. God does certain dispensational things that just don't fit into our plans or follow the normal pattern. When He does, He makes sure that there aren't any loose ends dangling. He takes care of business on all sides.

'Giving me away in order to keep me' worked for our marriage. Charles had literally given me away time after time when he really wanted me at home with him. Just like any normal husband, he experienced loneliness when I was away for days and sometimes weeks at a time. But when I came home, we experienced freshness in our relationship. It was always, "I can hardly wait to get back home because I know it's going to be like another honeymoon." One of the poems I've written about that experience goes like this:

"Knowing that I'm coming back
is the salve that eases the
pain of leaving you."

Before Charles and I married, I wrote to my mom and asked her what she thought about our getting married. She told me something I've shared with people contemplating marriage. First, we assume that you've prayed about it already and gotten what you believe to be the nod from God. But just because He gives you the "OK" doesn't mean you'll be free from trouble. No marriage is trouble-free, but you have the assurance that as you face those situations, you're not facing them alone. The Lord is with you.

Everyone who's ever gotten married has taken a chance. How things work out depends on the two of you, whether you're able to accept certain things about each other and tolerate the friction of differing convictions long enough to let it smooth you both out. I cannot overemphasize the need for Godly marital counseling.

As time went on, it became harder and harder for Charles and Danniebelle to keep their marriage alive. The two seemed to drift apart, and trust was broken by both parties. The couple separated in 1978. Charles moved out of the home. It was extremely hard on the family.

Danniebelle Reflects...

Charles seemed to be so engrossed in fixing cars because he thought I didn't really need him. I felt like I was being replaced by an overhead cam engine, broken drums that needed turning, distributor caps, plugs, points, rings, and valves. He thought I didn't need him, and I thought he didn't want me. I felt myself starving for attention, and instead of talking to him about it, I would talk to others.

Something else happened. I found myself drifting away from the things of the Lord. There was little or no time for devotion. Going to church was a routine calisthenic I practiced only because I knew I was supposed to. For what seemed to be a decade of nights, I lived so precariously on the edge of being out of fellowship with the Father, just humming along on my own, void of a sense of fulfillment and closeness to my husband.

It wasn't until I had sunken into an abyss of loneliness and tried to fill that void with meaningless relationships that I realized that my marriage had crumbled right before my eyes.

How had it all happened? Was there anything left to salvage? If I'd been as insightful as I thought I was, I could have foreseen the inevitable and possibly averted those ill winds. First, I should have recognized the strain caused by living with others and my husband under the same roof. Second, I failed to recognize and confess my need for the Holy Spirit's guidance and comfort in my everyday affairs.

Charles recognized the change in me but wasn't able to verbalize what was wrong. Finally, after hitting rock bottom, I was able to start the long climb back to wholeness. I began confessing and admitting my shortcomings to myself, God, and Charles. I began to sense the healing of the Holy Spirit. At first, I tried so desperately to convince Charles that I really loved him, despite my infidelity, and that as long as I lived, never would I allow our relationship to reach such a breaking point. Then I began to realize that I was trying too hard. Only time would heal the wounds we had inflicted on each other.

Would we be able to wait it out, or would the rest of our lives be spent tolerating each other? I'm not saying that I was totally at fault because, in most cases, when there is a rift, both parties are equally to blame. I had to admit my share.

LIFE ON THE ROAD – JUST DANNIEBELLE

In 1978, following the release of her solo albums, Danniebelle began touring on her own. Throughout her career, she traveled to over 75 countries, and similar to Andrae, her audiences were primarily white. In 1978, David Smallbone, concert promoter, father of the popular Christian pop-rock singer Rebecca St. James, and brother of the Christian pop duo, For King

& Country, arranged for Danniebelle to tour Sydney, Australia, and other provincial cities throughout the country.

One of the most memorable and beautiful concerts took place at the former William Balmain Teachers College in Lindfield, a suburb of Sydney. At that event, when Danniebelle joined with Christian artist Evie Tournquist, the spiritual energy was palpable as sunlight streamed through the tall windows.

During another visit to Sydney, as Danniebelle sang "His Eye Is On The Sparrow," the lighting engineer darkened the venue and had a thin spotlight on the piano. Danniebelle electrified the audience. Her testimony was powerful, and people sensed her sincerity as she expressed her love for the Lord.

In 1979, when Danniebelle's oldest daughter, Charlotte, was 18, she accompanied her mom on tour to the United Kingdom. The week-long tour extended to Birmingham, London, Bristol, Nottingham, and Wolverhampton and culminated with a huge festival featuring Danniebelle, along with British singer Cliff Richard and The Majestic Singers. During the concert, they sang "The Lord Is My Light" together with Danniebelle.

In 1981, when boxer Joe Louis passed away, Danniebelle sang "Bridge Over Troubled Water" at the funeral, and Rev. Jesse Jackson preached the eulogy. Celebrities in attendance included Frank Sinatra, Sammy Davis Jr., and several other high-profile personalities.

In 1982, Danniebelle traveled to Rome to sing for the Pope at the Vatican. Wintley Phipps, the Hawkins family, and Rev. Jesse Jackson also made the trip.

Danniebelle Reflects...

Well, this is definitely a day to remember. I got up at 7:30 AM. Yes, we are in Rome, Italy! After the continental breakfast, I sat in the Vatican courtyard to look at and listen to the Pope. He addressed the crowd of about 10,000 in Italian first, then in French, English, German, and Spanish. The Saint Bernardine Roman Catholic Church choir (all Black) from Baltimore, MD., sang, followed by Wintley Phipps and Arthur Seales from Chicago, who played the saxophone.

After the Pope's address, all of us sang "Kumbaya." Then, the Pope came to personally greet our group. I took pictures with the Pope shaking my hand.

Much of our time was spent preparing for a series of ministry gatherings at the Basilica of Santa Maria in Trastevere, an old 4th-century building definitely not made for amplified sound.

The first night, Father Good and Father Williams spoke. The crowd was moved. Then, Rev. Jesse Jackson spoke. Prior to Rev. Jackson's dynamic message, there were performances from Loretta Oliver, Arthur Seales (saxophone), Saint Bernadine Catholic choir, myself, Wintley Phipps, and Walter Hawkins and the Hawkins Family.

The second night was even more exciting than the first. The wife of the President of the Senate hosted us throughout the day. The crowds at the concerts were enthusiastic, and we all had a fabulous time. I'll never forget Rome!

I feel a sense of increased anointing of the Holy Spirit on the ministry. I treasure this above everything. I thank the Lord for his sense of being on course!

In 1983, Danniebelle left Light and Sparrow Records and signed with Onyx Records, where she worked with Gentry McCreary and Howard McCrary. That year, she recorded *Unmistakably Danniebelle*. All but two of the ten songs on the album were her compositions. "Beautiful People" was written by her long-time friend and road manager, Dora Taylor, and "I'm Not Here To Stay" was written by her dear friend, Michael Brown. In 1984, she received a Grammy nomination for Best Soul Gospel Performance for *Unmistakably Danniebelle*.

Danniebelle Reflects...

Had you even suggested to me that I'd be involved in a ministry that would have taken me to many different parts of the world, I would have told you how crazy you were. Now, I realize that the trip to California with Daddy was the launch of a new life for me.

When I was a little girl, I used to see different missionaries come from various parts of the world. I guess by the time they came to our church; they were worn out from the wear and tear of the mission field. They always seemed like people that were barely fed.

They were always grateful for anything they were given, and there seemed to be a glow in their eyes when they talked about where they'd been. My dream was to go to Africa. I just wanted to see the country.

Chapter Six

The Cankerworm

"Because of the Lord's great love we are not consumed, for his compassions never fail. They are new every morning; great is thy faithfulness." (Lamentations 3:22-23).

SOUTH AFRICAN BOYCOTT

In 1983, Henry Lowe of African Sunrise sponsored a South African tour featuring Danniebelle. Over a period of two weeks, she ministered in churches and small halls in Cape Town, Port Elizabeth, East London, Durban, and Johannesburg. The audiences were predominantly black, segregated, and underprivileged.

Little did she know, this trip would spark a series of devastating events that would plague her career for years to come. Danniebelle was among approximately one hundred American performers who were blacklisted and boycotted simply because they had traveled to South Africa.

The protest effort was organized by Unity in Action (UIC), an organization geared toward ending apartheid. UIC went as far as providing some of the artist's addresses and their managers' phone numbers to the United Nation's Center Against Apartheid. In October 1983, the group organized a demonstration against Danniebelle in front of the West Angeles Church of God in Christ. She was blindsided by the protests and hurt beyond belief.

In 1984, Danniebelle was nominated for an NAACP Image Award. However, UIC sent letters to the NAACP, informing them that Danniebelle was blacklisted and requesting that her nomination be withdrawn. They also threatened to boycott the awards show. The group's pressure paid off, and the NAACP withdrew the nomination.

In order to have her name removed from the blacklist, Danniebelle had to send the United Nations curator of the registry an admission of misjudgment and sign a pledge not to return to South Africa. Her name was finally removed from the registry; however, the damage had been done.

FOR RICHER OR POORER

Danniebelle suffered a considerable loss of income and a sharp decline in engagements due to the exposure of the boycott. In that same time period, her divorce from Charles became final. The combined impact of these events was extremely stressful.

> Danniebelle Reflects...

During the time that Charles and I were going through radical changes and separation, I found myself under a great deal of stress. I've always been a very quiet, well-balanced person. However, the separation did not fit logically into any place in my mind. I remember becoming very irate one minute and very calm the next. I tried to vent my feelings, but that went against the grain and fabric of my makeup. I'm not one who is given to arguing, so I did a lot of internalizing.

I wondered about the possibility of a congenial meeting to discuss the feasibility of reconciliation; however, the divorce proceeded and became final.

Everything wasn't perfect, but we came a lot closer to understanding and appreciating each other than ever before. It took a while, but we finally forgave each other and began accepting the fact that we were people with faults and under construction but with a strong desire to overcome our faults.

Sometimes it takes years to understand why things happen to you the way they do. My entire life was a giant step backward to make a giant leap forward.

My emotions were damaged, and I needed healing. I wasn't in any condition to help anyone else.

I began to see that even though there are lots of great things about the whole idea of traveling and gaining a reasonable degree of notoriety, that lifestyle can also be completely devastating. There are certain inalienable rights that you must be willing to forego if you are going to be at all accessible to the people who caused you to be who you are.

In a very real sense, you owe what you are to the public, and the public has a right to a part of you. If you're not willing to give of yourself, then you're in the wrong business.

I suppose it's that way in life. You realize that certain things you involve yourself in are really calculated risks, but you also know that if you don't take that risk, you won't know the joy and beauty of a new experience. Lots of people are afraid to give their life to Christ for that reason – afraid to risk the unknown, afraid that they might "backslide," afraid that someone might criticize them or not accept them.

To allow Christ through the power of the Holy Spirit to control your life is to allow yourself to be open to adventure. This does not say that you suddenly become risk-free or that everything you do from this point on is going to be without failure or disappointment, because these very elements cause us to learn the true meaning of trust.

The beauty is knowing that in every situation, whether adverse or pleasant, Jesus is with you.

THE BIG D

Danniebelle was taking medication for high blood pressure when she was diagnosed with Type 2 diabetes in November 1981. Both diseases require careful attention to one's diet.

Danniebelle Reflects...

There are a few areas of my life that need special attention. One is my spiritual diet, and another is my natural diet. Each of these areas requires constant monitoring and must be under the scrutiny of the Holy Spirit. When I slack up on Bible reading, prayer, and study of the Word, I tend to fall into an 'I don't care' attitude, which is detrimental.

I discovered that I had diabetes during my good friend Beverly Coy's visit. A group of us went to Las Vegas together. At that time, I was taking 250 milligrams of Diuril to combat my hypertension. I had been prescribed 50 milligrams by my physician, but I figured that if 50 milligrams was good, then 250 milligrams was better. I didn't realize that my self-medicating was harmful. As a result, I was always extremely thirsty. I drank gallons of apple juice on our way to Vegas, which forced frequent urination, rapid weight loss, blurred vision, and a loss of appetite and equilibrium. It was so bad that I couldn't walk from one place to another without extreme dizziness.

My blood sugar, which should have been around 100, was up to 287. When I got back home to California, I began dieting. Six months later, I had done so well that my blood sugar was back to normal. I was so delighted with my success that I got off the diet, but when I did, my sugar shot back up. Despite repeated attempts, I wasn't able to get it back down to that level.

Sometime in 1984, I began noticing an onset of numbness and pain in my feet, along with tightness and swelling.

I don't need this disease. I'm waiting for the manifestation of my healing, and until then, I'm taking glyburide (7.5 milligrams daily).

DRY MY WEEPING EYES

Things began to decline rapidly for Danniebelle. In 1984, a lien was placed on the house on the hill due to back taxes. Thankfully, with the help of the late Bishop Earnestine Cleveland-Reems and Dr. Christine Liddell, Danniebelle was able to secure an apartment in Hayward, California.

Shortly thereafter, in 1987, the Internal Revenue Service garnished her royalties. She had little to no income and could not keep the apartment. A good friend opened her home and allowed Danniebelle to stay with her.

God always makes a way out of no way.

In 1991, Danniebelle lost two people that meant the world to her within three months of one another. In October, her dearest friend, Bea Carr, her fellow group member from Andrae Crouch and the Disciples passed away, and in December her mother, Danniebell Jones passed. Mama Carter, the woman who had raised Danniebelle from age one to fifteen, had passed away ten years earlier.

Danniebelle Reflects...

Mama Carter died Friday, November 20, 1981, at Shadyside Hospital at about 5:00 PM. She was 89. I desperately wanted to get to Pittsburgh before she died, but it was impossible. During the last week of her life, I knew that she was holding on 'til I could come, but she couldn't wait any longer. She slipped away peacefully that Friday evening. I will miss her as long as I live, and I'm sure that every April 9th (that was her birthday), there will be a tear in my eye for the sweetheart who raised me.

Bea was killed in a tragic automobile accident in October. She's been one of my dearest friends. I feel a great sense of loss, but I know every time she sees me crying, she says, "Silly woman, why are you crying? You know how miserable I was, and you can only imagine how happy I am now! Quit crying and start rejoicing with me".

Mom died Sunday, the 1st of December, just a couple of months shy of her 81st birthday. She died peacefully while listening to "I Will Sing Holy" and "Freedom Bells."

Danniebelle could not attend her mother's funeral because she was hospitalized that Wednesday following her mother's passing after going to what she thought was a routine checkup.

Danniebelle Reflects...

The doctor checked my blood pressure, it was 200/130, and my blood sugar level was 300+. He immediately called the ambulance and rushed me into emergency. Somehow, I must have known he would send me to the hospital. I had my little bag with my bare necessities.

While in his office, I intimated the stress I had been under since mid-October. A lack of having received a paycheck, the recent death of my friend, the onset of nausea and vomiting, my mother's death, bills I had to pay, etc. No wonder, in addition to all of the tests he ordered, he sent the psychiatrist to see me in addition to all the tests he ordered. He even suggested that I might be suffering from depression.

Of course, I told the psychiatrist I didn't have time to be depressed. I just thought life went that way sometimes. The room they put me in was on a ward with mostly older people who had heart problems, among other maladies, so I was immediately hooked up to a heart monitor and an IV that fed me glucose, etc.

At first, I was the only one in the room, and then Bertha came into Bed A. She had a deep voice, and she spoke loudly because she was hard of hearing. She had serious respiratory problems, but she was a sharp 82-year-old white woman. She had a large family, but mainly a daughter, Betty, whose daughter loved her grandma a whole lot, came to see her every day, and brought her stuff she knew she liked. Betty didn't think her mom was going to be alive much longer, but the granddaughter treated her grandma as though she was going to be around forever. She brought her a poinsettia and wrote on the card, "to Grandma, you senile old bitch." Bertha loved it, but Betty was offended by it, so she hid the card in the drawer, but as soon as she'd leave, Bertha would pull it out and get the biggest laugh out of it.

When Bertha's minister came, I declared myself as part of the family, sort of the "black sheep," you might say, and they prayed with me, as well. I thought

I would only be in for a few days or so, but as time dragged on, it became apparent that I wouldn't be able to attend my mother's homegoing celebration. God whispered to my spirit: "Accept this." I knew it was more than my not attending the ceremony that I was to accept. Holy Spirit was telling me to embrace my whole circumstance. When I did that, I sensed an inner peace and joy that I cannot describe.

Sunday, they moved me to a smaller room with someone already in it. I hated it. But the Holy Spirit had already told me there was going to be someone I needed to share His love with, so I accepted it.

Noreen was a 67-year-old white lady who had lost a lot of weight rapidly, and they had done a series of tests to determine the cause. Monday afternoon, she was visited by a minister from her Catholic Church. I could tell Noreen wasn't much of a religious person; in fact, she didn't think too much of God. After all, He had not come through for her when she really needed Him. Her husband was an above-the-knee amputee as a result of an embolism. I noticed how negative Noreen was. If I'd wake up and say, "What a good day this is!" She'd say, "Yeah? Well, there's not much good about it." Then she'd go on to complain about all the things that had gone wrong for her.

When the minister came, she spoke such wonderful things about God's love and how much Jesus cared for Noreen. It was enough to melt the heart of the most hardened of all, but Noreen just cried and said how she didn't feel that God would ever forgive her for not following the rules of the church and how guilty she felt about having walked away from God.

While the minister was speaking to her, I prayed. After the minister left, God reminded me that there was someone that I was to share His love with, and Noreen was the one (or at least one of the ones). It just so happened that the little bag I had packed with my necessities was the same bag I had put two of the three coins I had been given years ago when I was at the Vatican in Rome. These coins held no particular value as far as I was concerned, but for some reason, I had managed to hold onto them through all of the different places I had moved into and out of. They had been blessed by the Pope and passed out to several of us who had gotten close enough to shake his hand after the group had sung for him.

I took one of those coins (it had the Pope's image on it) and told Noreen the story behind the coin, how I had acquired it, how the Pope had blessed it, and how God had orchestrated our being in the same room at the same time so he could personally demonstrate his love to her.

I told her the coin had no intrinsic value but that it was a symbol, a token to remind her of how much God really cared for her, and every time she looked at it, she would be reminded of two things: (a) God loved her, (b) He would never leave her.

Noreen was discharged the next day, but before she left, she told me with tears in her eyes how special a gift that coin was to her, and she'd never forget it.

Despite all Danniebelle was going through during this time, sharing God's love with others in their time of need is precisely what her ministry was about. She understood what it meant to be *"Ordinary People."*

Chapter Seven

Restoration

"And I will restore to you the years that the locust hath eaten, the cankerworm, and the caterpillar, and the palmerworm, my great army which I sent among you." (Joel 2:25)

BACK TO AFRICA

Danniebelle traveled back to Africa in August 1988, this time to Nigeria. I Care Ministries founder Scott Wesley Brown, and former Gospel Music Association President Steve Lorenz invited Danniebelle and other artists to participate in three days of conferences and concerts. The purpose was to equip the church with training, inspiration, encouragement, and instruments. Each artist brought their suitcases but had to have the other hand free to carry an instrument to give to the churches where they ministered.

Danniebelle, Kathy Hazzard, the late Billy Ingram, founder of Maranatha Community Church (Inglewood, California), and other artists spent two days in Nigeria and one day in Ghana. Though the people in Nigeria weren't exposed to a lot of gospel music from the West, they'd heard of artists like Andrae Crouch and Danniebelle.

During the first night of the concert, as Danniebelle was ministering and singing to a crowd of over 8000, she looked out at the massive crowd with tears in her eyes and said, **"I'm home!"** Everyone jumped out of their seats cheering. It was phenomenal. She had such a deep connection with the crowd.

The conference organizers expected 700 to 800 attendees but had over 3000. Several people walked from Ghana to Nigeria to attend the conferences, which were held in a church building with classrooms arranged in a semi-circle. Danniebelle led a class on vocals and had so many people that her class spilled over into the hallways. They all wanted to learn how to sing like Danniebelle. She'd sing a melody, "Ohhhh ohhhh ooooh ohh," and the whole class would repeat the melody, "Ohhhh, ohhhh ooooh ohh." They hung onto every little thing that she taught. They were hungry to learn the American gospel way.

Chief Ebenezer Obey, a well-known Nigerian Jùjú musician, opened the door for the group to do a concert in a public park. It was in a predominantly Muslim area, but the audience was huge, and the people loved it. Chief Obey was able to bridge the gap between both communities.

Danniebelle was so inspired by the experience and the multitude of worshipers praising God that she penned the song "O Se' Baba (Nigerian Praise)." She was also moved by the poverty she saw there. Along with others that were traveling, she emptied the entire contents of her suitcases sans undergarments and jewelry and gave everything to the people. When it was time for them to leave, all the artists donated their shoes, belts, pants, and dresses. They said to each other, "I can get another one of this, and I can get another one of that." Billy Ingram said, "We came full and left empty." But to coin the phrase another way, "They came full and left full."

Danniebelle Reflects...

We tend to want to see only the outwardly attractive and obviously beautiful because it offers no apparent assault to the physical senses and somehow has an emotional drawing power. We want to identify with and be associated with the "beautiful" as though by doing so, we are transformed into what we consider beautiful. We like the "successful."

Few of us actually seek out the less attractive and less beautiful. When confronted with it (such as the homeless, the alcoholic, the drug addict, or the slow learner), we turn away and choose not to minister whatever gifts we have to meet their needs. It is almost as though we feel we might be obligated to do something if we see it and not so obligated if we close our eyes. Maybe, we seem to think, after we blink, they'll be gone. So few of us understand the principle of giving.

HE KNOWS BEST

Speaking and ministering to the audience through her own testimony is one of the things that made Danniebelle's concerts so unique. During one concert, she shared a time when she was at home in her room and was feeling down. She'd been through so much with the divorce, and things were not meshing up financially. Just then, her son Charles walked in.

Just messing around, Charles grabbed the Bible on her dresser and said, "I am going to open this Bible to a random scripture, and you will have to tell me what book it is in."

Feeling the need to break out of her doldrums, she complied. He opened the Bible, and landed on a scripture, reading, "Fear thou not; for I am with thee: be not dismayed; for I am thy God: I will strengthen thee; yea, I will help thee; yea, I will uphold thee with the right hand of my righteousness" (Isaiah 41:10).

"Well son," Danniebelle said, "that would be in the book of Isaiah."

Intrigued by her knowledge of the Bible, he flipped to another scripture and read, "Truly my soul waiteth upon God: from him cometh my salvation. He only is my rock and my salvation; he is my defense; I shall not be greatly moved" (Psalms 62:1-2). "That's a good one, right?" he asked.

She nodded, sensing the Lord speaking to her situation through her son. "Yes, yes, that's a good one. That is in the book of Psalms."

"Okay, one more!" he said as he flipped through the pages. He read, "It is of the Lord's mercies that we are not consumed, because his compassions fail not. They are new every morning; great is thy faithfulness" (Lam. 3:22-23).

She began to play and sing "Great Is Thy Faithfulness." Danniebelle knew she had more to do for God's kingdom.

In 1985, Danniebelle joined Love Center in Oakland, CA, pastored by the late Walter Hawkins.

Danniebelle Reflects…

Great things are about to happen. I just know it. I just joined Love Center. I feel so good about my choice of church. I love Walter and Edwin, and I enjoy Walt's teaching. God is doing something phenomenal at Love Center. It's like He's gathering an army of people that the church world has rejected, and He's showcasing His glory through them. I love it!!

Danniebelle wrote the song "God Knows Best" recorded by Shirley Miller on her 1986 *I Must Go On* album. Edwin and Walter wanted Danniebelle to write something for Shirley because Danniebelle's style communicated such interpersonal sentiments.

In 1987, Danniebelle wrote, produced, arranged, played, sang, and recorded a musical collection on cassette titled *I Will Sing Holy*. She worked with Danny Hull and Engineer/Owner Tony Mills of Spark Studio in Berkeley, California.

That same year, the late Rev. Archie Dennis, founder of The Lord's Church (Pittsburgh, Pennsylvania), and his wife, Apostle Claudette Dennis, asked Danniebelle to come and serve as their Minister of Music.

Rev. Dennis and Danniebelle had a long association since both had been raised in sister churches in Pittsburgh. He belonged to NorthSide Church of God, while she had attended East Liberty Church of God. Danniebelle moved to Pennsylvania and stayed in that assignment until 1989.

In 1990, at the invitation of the late Rev. John Cherry, Danniebelle moved to Mitchellville, Maryland.

Danniebelle Reflects...

I moved to Maryland and joined Full Gospel AME Zion Church of Temple Hills in June, pastored by Rev. John Cherry. When I got there, I was so sick. Charles and Cheryl Phillips picked me up at the airport and brought me to the church. Pastor Cherry and his wife, Sister Diana, took me home, ministered to me, waited on me hand and foot, and allowed me to get into their jacuzzi.

They nursed me back to health, put me on staff and payroll, and found a place for me to stay. Brother Paul Henderson paid the largest portion of the rent, furnished the apartment, and got my peach leather sofa and loveseat.

The Cherrys were like a mother and father to me. They said God gave them a mandate to provide a place and space for me to heal physically, emotionally, and spiritually and provide an annuity that would make me financially solvent when retirement time came. In addition, they wanted to ease the pressure of me having to go and perform to earn money to pay bills.

A DESIGNER'S ORIGINAL

Danniebelle wanted to do another album, but nothing gelled. She had not recorded an album in eight years since *Unmistakably Danniebelle* was released in 1983. She was still reeling financially from the blow to her career from the boycotts, but her ministry and unyielding faith in God were steadfast. She heard the late Myles Munroe preach about purpose, and the seed was planted. Another seed was planted when Pastor Cherry preached "Finish" in May of 1991 during a Tuesday night Bible study. She told him that this particular message was for her.

That same day, she received a call from A&M Records. They were interested in recording a gospel album and heard favorable reports about Danniebelle. She went to River North Studios in Chicago to meet with music producer Joe Thomas and played some of her tunes. She had a track of several songs she'd been "pregnant" with for at least five years. They sat down and decided they would create the album *Designers Original*.

Danniebelle Reflects...

"Nigerian Praise" was to have a lot of drum sounds, nasal-sounding people with breathing voices, and some deep men's voices. "My Soul Loves Jesus" was to have an acapella old sound, fresh new modern chords, and a slick vocal sound. "No One Can Touch You Like Jesus Can" was to be a male/female duet. My brother, Archie Dennis, was appointed to sing with me.

Joe cried when I played "Jesus Knows Me" because it reminded him of his son, Mike. It was to be short and simple, just me and the Rhodes. "I Will Sing

Holy" was to have had an angelic choir on it, as well as "No One Can Touch You." Joe heard "He Knows Best" like a three-piece jazz band nightclub with a smoky feel. "Ain't No Devil in Hell" knocked everyone out, as did "Freedom Bells" He identified it as an "Elton John kind of song."

The title cut, "Designer's Original," was almost like a movie score with background vocals. I wanted a toe-tapper on there, kind of like Dorothy Norwood's "Victory is Mine." One day it came to me to do a medley including "Since Jesus Came Into My Heart," "Great Change in Me," and Carrie Gonzalo's "I'll Never Be the Same Again." Yes! That was it. I made several trips back and forth to Chicago. On or about the third trip, Joe had assembled Ralph Lofton (keyboard), Bob Leisig (bass), and Wayne Stewart (drums).

Joe secured a nice studio apartment for me, and every time I came into town, they'd have a limo pick me up from the airport. It dawned on me that they were treating me like a star. You can't imagine how that made me feel after having been virtually ignored by the Christian record industry for eight years.

Joe saw a potential that others who claimed to hear the voice of God had completely overlooked. Of course, the enemy got mad and tried to pull a few tricks. But every time he tried something, God would give me something else fresh and new that would only enhance the vitality of the album, like the rap on "Ain't No Devil In Hell." This was to be the reprise. Joe resisted the idea because he felt that mine was too much of a class act to degrade it with rap. But I knew God had given it to me to be an encouragement to the body of Christ. That was the last thing I did. It was as though God had orchestrated the whole album.

Against all odds, I was determined to finish this album like Pastor Cherry had preached. On Sunday, February 2, 1992, at about 5:00 pm, I said Amen, and that was that! I was thoo' (through)! Around here, when we thoo', we say 'Amen, and thank you, Jesus!'

SISTER SERCER DOES GMWA

Rev. James Cleveland's Gospel Music Workshop of America (GMWA) was an annual event where singers, songwriters, choirs, preachers, and national performers met to advance African American Gospel music. Rev. Cleveland had recorded "Ordinary People" in 1978, and he and Danniebelle were good friends.

Following the release of *Designer's Original*, Danniebelle attended GMWA in 1992.

Danniebelle Reflects...

This past week was spent at the Gospel Music Workshop of America in Chicago, headquartered at the Chicago Hilton. This was the first workshop since Rev. James Cleveland died, and by all accounts, it was the most successful. So many people were there. It was most gratifying to have been stopped by so many different people in the lobby who each had a different story of what my music meant to them. We won't know the full impact of the ministries God has given us until eternity, but every artist needs to receive some of that kind of love.

So many people expressed how they loved "O Se' Baba" on the new album. A lot of the radio announcers told me how they got requests for it all the time. CGI records hosted a reception during the workshop, which was well-attended.

While in Chicago, I learned that Carolyn Simmons, a great singer from Houston, Texas, had died. Also, I learned of the passing of Ralph Weekes, a brother who lived in London and had sponsored me on several occasions in many of the cities in England. Thomas Whitfield had also recently died.

Andrae and Sandra were at GMWA, and when Richard Smallwood sang "It Will Be Sweet When We Meet," they had to leave the room. Mother Crouch had just died in April, and I could feel what they were feeling. Richard sang so beautifully; it stirred such emotions. Tramaine was there, as well as Vanessa Bell, who wore us all out with "Peace Be Still." She is so gifted. John P. Kee walked away with so many awards, and he deserved them all. I was especially impressed with the enthusiasm and excellent musicianship of the young people. They were so good. The list of artists read like a who's-who in gospel music.

Danniebelle as Sister Sercer

Before Tyler Perry made Madea popular, Danniebelle did stand-up comedy. She'd stuff her bottom lip with paper towels, wear an old dress, shoes, wig, and an old mother's church hat, and carry a large vinyl purse. Her "piano-ist," Isolevia Viselia Dunkin, played by Danniebelle's good friend Bishop Yvette Flunder would accompany Sister Sercer. Danniebelle performed her routine at the Gospel Music Workshop of America, and many in the audience did not realize it was Danniebelle. She introduced herself as Sister Sercer - and spelled it out, emphasizing the letter "R." "I'm Sister Sercer, that's spelled S-E-R(ah)-C-E-R(ah)"

"God gives me many gifts! He gives me the gift of stirring confusion everywhere I go."

"As a little girl, I used to play marbles...but then I read in the Bible where it said, "Marble not!" The crowd roared with laughter.

"I have several different gifts. One of my gifts is opening up the Bible. I can open up the Bible, and what-son-e-ver my finger falls on, that's my scripture for the day." (She opens a Bible)

"..And Judas went and hanged himself...Wait, I don't think that's one of em." (She turns to another page)

RESTORATION

"...Go down and do likewise," "...It ain't working right!"

"OK. Last one." "..Whatever thou do, do it quickly."

By this time, the audience is in tears with laughter.

She went on, "God healed me from five diseases. I'll tell you what they were. They were canSUH, high blood preSHUH, SHUGAH diaBEETEEES, heart trouble, and wait...." (Trying to recall the list again, counting on her fingers and mumbling under her breath...)

"canSUH, high blood preSHUH, SHUGAH diaBEETEEES, heart trouble, ...Now, what was that other one?"

"Oh!" She exclaimed. "It was my MIND. I kept forgetting things!"

The audience loved it!

THE BEST GETS BETTER

In 1995, Danniebelle released *The Best Gets Better*, where she rearranged and rerecorded some of her most popular songs.

Danniebelle Reflects...

There was not the fanfare as with "Designers Original," however, it was significant to me in that "I Go To The Rock," "Ordinary People," and "Mary Had a Little Lamb" were included on it as well as some new tunes, including

"You Deserve the Best," and "Garment of Praise," written by Charles Smith from Cliff Turner's church in Chicago.

Danniebelle continued to book small engagements when and where she could, though traveling was getting harder and harder. She'd sell her music after her events, and often the venue would take up a love offering.

Danniebelle Reflects…

That year, I was invited to North Augusta, South Carolina, to minister at a conference. It just happened to be where my daughter Cynthia, her husband Lance, their children Boo (that's Little Lance's nickname), Cedric, Vanessa, and Cindy's in-laws, Francis and Granny live.

The service on that Saturday night was excellent. People said they were blessed. They raised an offering of $200 and bought my tapes and CDs. They put me up at the Sheraton and treated me royally.

My friends Hassan and Miriam Fawaz had arranged for me to sing at their church, Whole Life Ministries (Augusta, Georgia), pastored by Sandra Kennedy, that Sunday morning. I thought I would only sing a few songs, but the pastor said she felt led by God to give me the whole service. The people bought every tape I had, and the pastor gave me a check for $350.00. Again, the people said they had been blessed. One mother, whose son had just gotten out of prison the week before, shared with me that every word I said had such relevance and that her son gave his heart to the Lord that day. It was a great service.

Chapter Eight

The Final Years

"Behold, what manner of love the Father hath bestowed upon us, that we should be called the sons of God: therefore the world knoweth us not, because it knew him not. Beloved, now are we the sons of God, and it doth not yet appear what we shall be: but we know that, when he shall appear, we shall be like him; for we shall see him as he is." (1 John 3:1-2)

THIS ROBE OF FLESH

Beginning in 1995, Danniebelle was no longer able to travel. Though her faith in God never wavered, her health began to take a serious turn.

Danniebelle Reflects...

I've been in and out of the hospital several times. It started in January 1995 in Dallas, Texas, because of seizures. E.K Bailey asked me to come minister at Concord Baptist Church; he was considering me for the music ministry at his church. I flew down, and as usual, we went to a restaurant for dinner that Sunday after service. I had seafood, and as I went back to the hotel, I noticed I had difficulty walking. I had trouble planting my feet, but I didn't think anything of it. That was all I remembered. When I woke up, I was in intensive care. Of course, I wanted to know why I was there. They told me I'd had several seizures.

The next time I had a seizure was at the BWI airport, on the way to a program in Greenville, SC, for Nancy Wilson. While waiting to board, I didn't feel good, much like the time I had seizures before. I woke up in Saint Agnes Hospital in Baltimore. My blood pressure was 200/120, and I was on all kinds of medication. It was having an adverse effect on my kidneys.

In August 1995, my kidneys shut down completely, and after a renal angiogram, my doctor put me on dialysis. I was being treated at the Kidney Care center in Largo, MD., with Continuous Ambulatory Peritoneal Dialysis

(CAPD). I had to sit in the dialysis chair for 3 1/2 hours every Tuesday, Thursday, and Saturday.

During this time, my income went down to nothing. I had no way of keeping up with anything. I told Sister Diana Cherry about my circumstances. She told me not to worry and that they would take care of everything for me. Since July or August of 1995, they have paid my rent, car note, and phone bill. I have no idea how long I'll have to depend on John and Diana Cherry, and I never thought it would come to this, but I am so grateful for them.

In order to do CAPD, I had to have a catheter surgically inserted into my abdomen. That was done by Doctor Ray in the Annapolis Medical Center. Surgery was scheduled for September, but just as I was going in for surgery, I had a slight pain in my right groin area. Doctor Ray said he would check it out during surgery. When he did, he discovered my appendix had ruptured, and there was a hidden abscess beneath it. When I recovered from the anesthesia, he told me that he had removed the abscess, but I was in excruciating pain. It took me a while to recover.

As I look back, I realize that if I had not been on the operating table at that particular time, I could have died. But God! He has me here for a purpose, and I want to fulfill that purpose. I'm feeling stronger day by day. The blood pressure and blood sugar levels are down. I eat almost anything I want, and I've lost about 25 pounds. I haven't been able to get to church like I want to, and I spend a lot of time resting in bed. I now do my CAPD four times a day. I'm on Social Security, but I'm still writing songs.

In 1997, Danniebelle moved from Mitchellville, Maryland, to Fremont, CA., to be close to her family. She moved in with her daughter, Charlotte, son-in-law Michael, and their three children, Charisse, Michelle, and Melinda. She was also closer to her son Charles and grandson Cameron.

Shortly before the move, she received devastating news from the doctor.

Danniebelle Reflects…

The doctor came to the house in Maryland and told me I had cancer in my left breast. He said I needed to have a simple mastectomy. I opted to have it done in California. My daughter, Charlotte, sisters Agnes, Cynthia, Paula, and brother Bill were at the hospital with me.

Soon after the mastectomy, my left leg had to be amputated because of the sore on my left heel that had turned gangrenous. When I came out from under anesthesia after the amputation, all I wanted was to see my family.

Rehabilitation for Danniebelle following the amputation of her leg was difficult. At one point, she all but shut down mentally and physically. Following the surgery, she was not complying with anyone at the rehabilitation facility. Her dear friends, Sandra Crouch and Carol Houston, received a call from Danniebelle's sister, Paula.

They decided to fly from Southern California to see her. No one knew they were coming. They told the people at the rehab facility they were her sisters from Los Angeles. When they entered the room, Danniebelle was sitting in a chair with her stump elevated and her head down. She was depressed and had given up. She was ready to die.

The anointing of God hit Sandra and Carol so hard against the demonic forces that wanted to take Danniebelle out. They began praying, "You shall live and not die! God is not through with you yet."

They said, "Yes, the leg is gone, but the anointing and the ministry you are here to give is not over. It's not over until God says, 'That's it!'"

The anointing was powerful.

Sandra noticed a small keyboard in the closet and placed it on Danniebelle's lap, and when Danniebelle began to play the keyboard, her whole attitude changed.

They finished praying and visiting with their sister-friend and flew back to Los Angeles. The folks at the rehab facility asked Paula, "Who were those sisters?"

God used Sandra and Carol to change the atmosphere. Danniebelle seemed to blossom after that day.

Danniebelle Reflects...

Thank you, Father, for how you brought me back from death's door two years ago. When the doctors said I had only nine more months to live, you said, "Not so!" Whose report do we believe? We shall believe the report of the Lord. As long as I have breath in this body, I'll tell others of your mercy, grace, and faithfulness. You are my Lord!

Yours, Danniebelle Hall

WE LOVE YOU, DANNIEBELLE

In February 1997, Rebecca Matthews spearheaded an appreciation fundraiser service for Danniebelle at Bishop Yvette Flunder's church, City of Refuge in San Francisco. Bay Area radio personality Sheila Robinson hosted the event. Danniebelle saw lots of friends she'd not seen in years. Many gospel greats attended and performed Danniebelle's songs. Shirley Miller sang "God Knows Best," Lawrence Matthews, Tina Watson, and Edwin Hawkins sang "Ordinary People," Bishop Yvette Flunder and Dr. Bobby Lyons sang "I Go to the Rock," Patrisha Gill, a long-time friend, and mentee of Danniebelle, played the piano while the choir sang. Mayor Willie Brown proclaimed July 21, 1997, *Danniebelle Hall Day* in San Francisco, California.

In 1998, Danniebelle joined South Bay Community Church in Fremont, California founded by Pastor Stanley Long. He felt impressed by God to take care of Danniebelle in her final years, and that's what they did. Danniebelle did not want to be treated like a celebrity, she just wanted to be accepted and loved.

While living with her daughter Charlotte, and son-in-law Michael, her son Charles and other church members would come to the house and physically pick her and her wheelchair up and take her down the three flights of stairs so she could go to dialysis two to three times a week. Once dialysis was done, they'd meet ParaTransit and carry her back upstairs. Eventually, the church found placement for her in an assisted living facility (St. Regis).

Danniebelle Reflects...

The entire church is taking me on and caring for me. Their first objective was to get me out of Charlotte's, mainly because it presented a safety hazard because of the stairs. Pastor Long headed the whole campaign. The entire staff became involved. This included Assistant Pastor Alyse Orbih, Margaret Maxwell, Denise Churchill, Donnie Roberts, and Dayrll Lewis. The church housed me in an assisted living setting at Saint Regis retirement center in Hayward, California. We're contacting the people I have ministered to over the past 30 years, asking them to consider sharing in the cost. Jehovah Jireh will provide.

Gracious Father, thank You for Your greatness and Your faithfulness. You have provided all I have ever needed. I have no idea what lies ahead, but I know You hold all of my tomorrows in Your hands.

I trust You to order my steps and my stops. I do indeed take delight in Your lordship over me. You are sovereign. I love You for this place You have me in now because I can praise and sing to You as long and as loud as I want. I know. You love it!

Your maidservant, Danniebelle

Once she was settled at St. Regis, Danniebelle gained independence, especially after getting her motorized wheelchair. She petitioned the staff to consider adding her to the payroll as a "resident counselor" for the elderly.

She led a weekly Bible study and ministered to the residents. Many of them prayed the prayer of salvation and accepted Christ as their personal savior.

Her son, Charles, would visit to engage in their favorite pastime, Othello! Danniebelle's mind was not as sharp as in earlier years, so it was somewhat bittersweet for Charles.

Danniebelle sang on a song called "Thank You," the title track for songwriter, and musician Christal Robert's CD Sampler on Monterey Bay Records. Danniebelle was a wonderful friend, mentor, and encourager for Christal.

This recording would be Danniebelle's last.

MR. CHARLES E. HALL

In May 1998, Danniebelle flew to Pittsburgh for Archie Dennis' Believers Conference, which is usually held on Memorial Day weekend.

Danniebelle Reflects...

Pastor Cherry sent for me (First Class, if you please!). Prophetess Juanita Bynum was the keynote speaker. She comes out of the gate bad! She's dynamite! I had the rare privilege of prophesying to the prophetess. That was a real treat.

My cousin, Naomy Tallon, and her husband Lawrence were gracious hosts. Archie came over to Naomy's on the Monday after the convention and brought some fried chicken. We were about halfway through the meal when I got a call from my daughter, Charlotte, informing me that her father, Charles Emile Hall, had died. He died from complications of diabetes.

Later, I learned that Charlotte had planned for Archie to be at the house when she called so that he could comfort me. That was divine wisdom for me to have been on the East Coast when he died. Can't you just see me going to his homegoing, boohooing, snotting, and carrying on?

One of the most remarkable things about Charles was his tremendous sense of humor. I recall when he didn't know the words to a song, he made up his own like, "What a fellowship, what a Georgia Brown, leaning on the everlasting arms!"

Previously, I'd had the privilege of sharing Jesus Christ with Charles. Of course, everyone in the church had been witnessing to him, but I told him that if he wanted to be with me, he'd have to come to church.

His conversion to Christ was dramatic. However, he demanded that I show him in the Bible where it said, "Thou shalt not smoke." I explained that once he gave his life to Christ, that old desire to smoke would just be taken away. Finally, on June 27th, 1958, he surrendered totally and without reservation to the Lord with a willingness to be taught in the things of the Lord. This was typical of Charles. Whatever he was into, he was in it all the way, wholeheartedly.

Even after our divorce, he tried to direct my life in his own way. I realize now that this was his way of showing his concern. I honestly felt that it was the stress brought on by the divorce that triggered my diabetes, which brought on hypertension, which was the cause of the kidney failure. I had, in essence, blamed him. But after I really thought about it, I realized that it was due to carelessness on my part. Charles didn't accept my theory that it was his fault. When I was in the hospital, he didn't want to come and see me. I later learned that it wasn't that he didn't want to see me; he just didn't want to see me with all those tubes and I.Vs.

Chapter Nine

Letters From Danniebelle

LETTERS FROM DANNIEBELLE

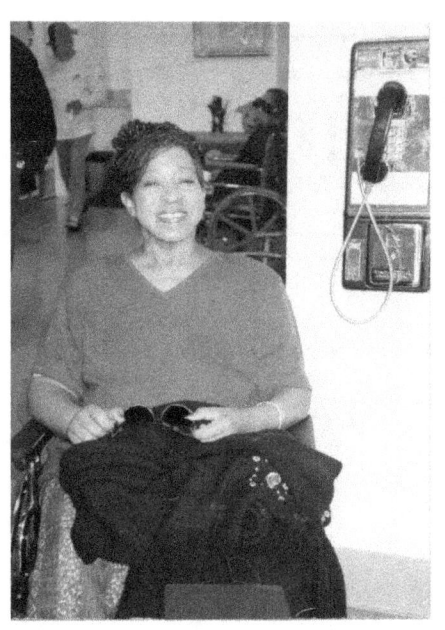

Danniebelle at St. Regis

In April of 2000, Danniebelle's daughter, Cynthia, built a website for her mother (www.danniebelle.com). Danniebelle wrote letters outlining her physical challenges and letters of encouragement to her many devoted fans that visited the website. They, in turn, could post comments on the message boards. Little did anyone know that we were witnessing the last nine months of Danniebelle's life on Earth.

April 6, 2000

Some of you may have heard that I have been hospitalized. Thank you for your prayers and concerns.

As you know, I am on hemodialysis. In hemodialysis, blood is pumped from the body to a filter. The blood is purified and returned to the body. One of the disadvantages of hemodialysis is dialysis graft failure.

I have been faced with how to keep my shunt and my permacath open. You see the shunt is my lifeline to being able to purify my blood. For some unknown reason, I clot easily, so as a backup system, I have a permacath installed in my chest.

The past few weeks have been spent in and out of the hospital trying to open up my shunt. That has been unsuccessful, and eventually, I will have to have another shunt placed in the left arm. In the meantime, the permacath keeps clotting, and as a last resort, the doctors inserted a catheter in the groin.

Obviously, your prayers have been working because the upside is - I am out of the hospital. Through all of this, my spirit has remained undaunted. I'll go a step further. I am actually rejoicing in the Lord at how good I feel. There are some days that I don't feel as though I have ever been sick. As a matter of fact, I feel better now sometimes, than I did when I thought I was feeling great. I thank you again for your prayers.

Love Danniebelle

April 13, 2000

When I went to dialysis on Saturday, they were not able to exchange my blood through my permacath. This is a very frustrating situation. I immediately knew that I would have to go to the hospital. The nurses tried everything they could to open up the port. They tried to loosen the clot, but that didn't work either. By this time I was desperate. I knew that I had to be dialyzed. The only option was to get a femoral catheter placed in my groin. However, this is a temporary option, it will only work while lying in the hospital. That dialysis proved to be very successful.

The process was very painful in and of itself. I had a lot of scar tissue in that area from a previous right popliteal angioplasty. This opens up the veins in the right leg. As you can guess by now, I have some circulatory problems. Let me *just say a word to those of you who are feeling immortal, please take good good care of yourself while you are young. This does not ensure you a long life, but it at least ensures the quality of your life. Be careful of your diet, get plenty of exercise, drink proper amounts of fluids, and lay off the salt.*

The doctor's plan was to transfer me to another hospital where he could put a shunt in my left arm, this turned out to be unsuccessful, so they inserted another permacath. It worked, and I was able to be dialyzed.

The upside of all of this is that while I was in the hospital, I happened to watch The Bobby Jones Gospel Show. I heard John P. Kee sing a song that blessed me out of my sock!!! (Remember, she only had one leg). I can understand those of you that write me and tell me how my songs have ministered to you. I just want to say John; you have blessed me more than you'll ever know. If anyone reads this, and talks to John, please tell him this for me.

Isn't it amazing how songs can carry you through circumstances? I can recall when my leg was first amputated, all I could hear in my spirit was Walter Hawkins' song "When The Battle Is Over" There was a period of time when I was going through extreme nausea and vomiting, and it seemed as though the doctors couldn't determine what was wrong with me. Rosie Wallace's song "Jesus Doeth All Things Well." I hummed that and sang that in my mind over and over, and God brought me through that time of discomfort.

I am out of the hospital. The doctors still have not determined how they are going to proceed, but all is well. Plans for the future: To put my name on the list for a new kidney, and watch as God opens up that door. Thank you for your prayers.

Love Danniebelle

April 27, 2000

I just want to thank you all for praying me through these last couple of weeks of dialysis. For a moment, I thought I was going to have to go back into the hospital. Thanks to your prayers and a lot of technical savvy, the permacath that I have installed has opened up. I was able to have a successful dialysis. Whenever the nurse would start the machine, I would put my hand over my mouth and pray in the Spirit. I really didn't care if the nurses heard me. All I wanted was to break through and ask the Lord to dialyze successfully.

I just went to the doctor this week (Neurosurgeon) He seems to feel that it is best to leave things status quo because of my restricted blood vessels. We will probably delay any surgery for a little while. Actually, we are trying to buy a little time to give my body a little rest. The last thing that I want to do is to go onto CAPD (Peritoneal dialysis) I have been there, and done that. I would like to think that I have moved on. Peritoneal dialysis does have its advantages. I don't have to restrict my fluids as much, and don't have to have such a strict diet. We all know how I love to eat.

Speaking of eating, we just got a Krispy Kreme Donut franchise in town. Every opportunity I get, I go out there to buy donuts for the staff here at the retirement facility of course. Just pray for me.

I have really focused in on our bible study. We are continuing in Genesis. We broke away during the Easter season to contemplate trial, crucifixion, death, burial, but most of all resurrection.

I have my life and my family, and I can honestly say that I am happier than I have been in my whole life. I am doing what God wants me to do. It is most fulfilling to be obedient to the Lord.

If I were to quote a song, it would be "Trust and obey, for there's no other way to be happy in Jesus but to trust and obey."

Love Danniebelle

May 27, 2000

It's time for an update. We are going to update monthly rather than weekly. On the last update, dated April 27, 2000-the doctors wanted to delay surgery to allow my body to heal. Also, I was hoping that I would not have to go back to CAPD (Continuous Ambulatory Peritoneal Dialysis), but with all of the trouble that I was having with the fistula clogging-it was inevitable. I had the surgery about 3 weeks ago. Let me tell you the difference between Hemodialysis and Peritoneal dialysis.

Hemodialysis is done at a Dialysis Center. The patient is hooked up to an artificial kidney with lines that circulate and cleanse the blood. Peritoneal dialysis is a process done at home. A catheter was installed to accept a solution suspended from an IV pole. The solution drains into the peritoneal lining, and sits there for a while. It is released, filtering out the toxic wastes. I have to do this four times a day on a regular schedule. The whole process takes about half an hour. It is of utmost importance that this is done in a sterile environment. I had to take classes to learn how to do this correctly. If done incorrectly, an infection can enter my body. I will begin CAPD as soon as my body has healed from the surgery.

I can feel myself healing. Now I can turn and move without groaning. I'm finding that having something to look forward to gives me impetus, it keeps the juices flowing. Life has such meaning to me. I'm enjoying cooking for myself. I do get frustrated because it takes me so long to do anything.

The thought of doing Peritoneal dialysis is just a bit frightening. I'm hoping I will have the strength to do it. I've done it before but five years ago. I was a different person then. Not necessarily better, just different. My final answer on CAPD is I CAN DO IT. I can do ALL things through Christ, which strengthens me. That's my final answer.

Bible study is steadily growing. We're progressing through Genesis. Our last study focused on the fourteenth chapter. We honed in on Abraham's giving tithe to Melchizedek. We cross-referenced to Malachi 3:10 and pointed out that God does not want us to give him what's left over after we pay our bills and do whatever we want to do. He wants to be first. He wants us to give him preeminence in all things. Like Kim Burrel says in her song "I Come To You More Than I Give" If you show me your canceled checks, I can tell you where your heart is. It's about investing in the Kingdom of God and being a wise steward over what God entrusts in our hands.

Prayer requests: Strength to do CAPD, the flow of God's creativity through me to write songs, the opening of doors in terms of TV programs that will help promote the ministry God has given me, and the strength to walk through those doors. The Holy Spirit just reminded me of Isaiah 43:18 and 19. Praise you, Jesus!!!

Love you always, Danniebelle

June 17, 2000

Hello all. I realized it was time for another update. I guess I was waiting for something eventful to happen. Then I realized that my being alive and breathing was an event enough for me to rejoice over.

The CAPD (Continuous Ambulatory Peritoneal Dialysis) classes are coming along well. Even though I've been through it before, it's like learning the steps all over again. Last time (5 yrs ago) I was on the Baxter system. Now I'm on the Fresenius system. Oh yes, on hemodialysis only 3 times a week instead of four. I've got about two more weeks of hemo. It takes a lot longer for me to get stuff through my head. The last class I had was on a hemo day, it was hot, and my instructor's voice began sounding like a little mosquito whipping around my ears. Toward the end of the class (which lasts 4 hours at a time, 2 x a week) I just broke down and cried. I guess it was a combination of it being hot, Mary's voice, not having had any breakfast, and basically being sick and tired of being sick and tired. It all culminated in my crying like a baby.

After class, I went out and got an ice cream cone. Not just any old ice cream cone but Snickers ice cream. I deserved it. I sat outside and savored every minute of the ice cream, spitting out the peanuts for some deserving bird's meal. It's really difficult to control my fluid intake during the hot summertime. I limit myself to 5 eight-ounce glasses a day. It's hard, but I'm doing it. Oh yeah, I baked some teriyaki chicken thighs; oooh so good- got to build up my protein level.

Prayer requests:
Pray that I'll have the physical strength to do CAPD.
Pray that God will send more people to bible studies.
Pray that I'll get going on my book.
Pray that God's creativity will flow into me so I'll write more songs. and
Pray that God will send me a companion.

I think I'd like to have one. I guess I've really not looked in that direction since the passing of Charles. He has such huge shoes to fill. Actually, whoever God sends has to be his own person. I've got to accept him, plus he's got to accept me like I am. Being the perfectionist that I am, that ain't easy, with all my other idiosyncrasies. Contrary to popular opinion, I'm not an easy person to live with. Just ask my children if you don't believe me. Long list huh, but God knows my heart, and now you know too. More than anything, I want to keep my ear close to God's mouth so I'll be sensitive and obedient to his voice. He is preeminent in my life.

Our recent bible study was in Genesis 17. The key thought was how Abraham obeyed God. Even though Abraham didn't know anything about circumcision, God had established that every male be circumcised. The key phrase is in verse 23. The selfsame day as God had said unto him

May you and I hasten to obey the voice of the Lord. God gives us the vision; we come up with the plan to implement that vision. Just be sure it's God speaking to you and that it's not the residual of those collard greens, yams, and fried chicken you ate and laid down on and had a cornbread vision (or could it have been the baked beans?)

Love you so much, Danniebelle

July 20, 2000

This has been a fantastic week. My baby girl, the creator of my web page, has come to visit me from South Carolina. I don't know when it happened, I just know that I'm the baby and she's the mommy. If she could, she'd run my life from 3,000 miles away. She came out this week with no particular agenda, just to visit her mom and make sure I'm behaving, as I should.

Physically, I sense a real improvement in my condition. I decided, with my doctor's approval, to quit taking a lot of the medications. He agreed. Some of it I was taking for conditions that had existed a long time ago, such as an appetite enhancer. Truth is, I had started eating everything in sight!!! I'm not a health food nut, but I'm becoming more conscientious about what I put into my body. After all, it is the temple of the Holy Ghost.

Spiritually, I'm up!! I just came through a testing time. My leg had swollen. I was retaining fluid, and my podiatrist gave me such bad news. I thought I was going to have to go into the hospital. Then I got two months behind on my rent. The enemy wanted me to worry over how it was going to get paid and worry about my swollen leg. God assured me He'd take care of both situations.

He reminded me that HE had provided for me and healed me all these years. Why should he stop now?? Trust me. No, trust HIM. He's an on-time God. Yes, he is.

The bible studies are going well. Pray that God will touch the hearts of the residents and that I'll be faithful to what he's called me to do, even when it seems non-productive. He promised if we would be faithful over a few things, he would make us rulers over many.

Love you so much, Danniebelle

August 3, 2000

Let me tell you a little story. You might want to call it an update, but I call it how God answers the smallest prayer. It was about 2:30 am early Thursday morning. I was listening to Family Radio, KEAR as I do most early mornings. The Bible reading was in Genesis. As you know, we've been reading in our bible study about Abraham and Isaac.

Let me also say that you know I've been doing CAPD, which requires an absolutely antiseptic environment. It was about 2 am, and I had just done an exchange. I was about to settle down to listen to the radio when I heard that horrible zinging sound that mosquitoes make. I was totally annoyed. No flies, bugs, mosquitoes, or critters of any kind were allowed in my environment.

My prayer was Lord, let me kill that pest. You know my eyes aren't as keen as they used to be, so make me a sharpshooter. Let me locate that sucker and kill him". (Don't ask me why it's a male mosquito, I just know it was).

As I prayed, I sat up, turned on the light, looked on the wall above my head, and there he was perched above me. I rolled up my Essence magazine, and in the same style that David released the stone from his slingshot into Goliath's head, I swatted that mosquito. BAM-he was dead. You probably would have laughed, but there I was sitting on the bed clapping my hands in victory and praising the Lord for coming through for me.

God is gracious, I'm feeling good, and I marvel at his provision. He's an on-time God-yes he is. Thank you for your love and your continued prayers. See you on the web page.

Love you so much, Danniebelle

August 30, 2000

It is time for another update. This time, I decided to focus on the good things that are happening - and there are so many.

When I was originally faced with doing peritoneal dialysis, I hated the idea because I didn't feel I had the strength or the discipline to do it. As time goes on, I find not only do I have the strength, but I am feeling much better these days. I'm even spending more time in the kitchen cooking for myself.

I thank God for the people working here. For the most part, they're so very helpful. If I were to live in my own home and had to pay for the services that are provided, it would amount to much more than the monthly rent I have to pay.

Every month, I have to trust God to provide the $2,000.00 I need to meet my monthly budget. So far, he's been faithful. I've been praying that God would fix my situation so that I wouldn't be concerned about finances.

This is me thanking God for my family. This month, two of my sisters came over, and we spent the entire afternoon singing, laughing, praying, and crying. Remembering from where God had brought me.

God is restoring some of my piano playing ability that was lost when I had the stroke in '95. I still find it difficult to play and sing at the same time due to the lack of breath control, but I'm dealing with it.

I'm thankful that I have a renewed interest in deep-down meat-eating bible searching and I'm spending time learning features on my Casio CJ 541. I'm focusing on how to spark greater interest and attendance in the Bible studies. Perhaps you could suggest something I could do to encourage the residents to attend the studies.

Love you so much, Danniebelle

September 20, 2000

This is more of an update-lett.

In a few days, I will get the cycler - that's the peritoneal dialysis machine that will allow me to dialyze one - all night instead of four times a day. This will free me up during the day. Please pray for me that I'll be successful.

Love you, Danniebelle

P.S. - Thanks for the financial help. You're so precious to me!!

October 30, 2000

I've been writing this update for about a week, and it struck me that instead of writing events in my life, it would be better to use the format of writing a letter to God. Here goes.

Dear Father;

Thank you for the privilege of talking to you as Daddy; because that's who you are. You understand me like no other. I never want to presume on your holiness, but right now I just want to talk to you-child to Daddy.

Sometimes I've felt like you flat-out abandoned me what with all the pain and discomfort I seem to constantly face. Sometimes I wonder if you hear my cries and do you see my tears. Sometimes I wish you'd go on and call me home.

Then I wake up the next morning and realize you've spared me here for a purpose and that you are true to your word, "I will never leave you nor forsake you. Trust Me. I see the entire tapestry, my child, you only see a thread of the rug. I'm using every situation that your faith in me will be increased. I've brought you this far, I'll carry you all the rest of the way".

I thank you, Lord, for having this little talk with you. I feel better now. Really when I look at it, I have everything I need and some of the things I want. All is well no matter what I see or hear from the doctor, all is well. I love you,

Danniebelle

Chapter Ten

Well Done

"O give thanks unto the Lord; call upon his name: make known his deeds among the people. Sing unto him, sing psalms unto him: talk ye of all his wondrous works." (Psalm 105:1-2).

THY GOOD AND FAITHFUL SERVANT

Danniebelle was admitted to the hospital in November 2000. The toes on her remaining foot were gangrenous. Doctors planned to amputate these toes to eliminate the gangrenous portions of her right lower limb, as well as an angioplasty on her remaining leg to try to improve circulation.

Before the surgery began, things took a turn for the worse, and her heart stopped. She was resuscitated; however, she became unresponsive. Doctors did not expect her to last through the night.

Pastor Stanley Long visited Danniebelle the day before she passed. He recalled that she was asleep when he walked into the room, but he felt the undeniable presence of God. Visiting and praying for people in the hospital was nothing strange for him, but he felt God's presence at a greater level on this occasion. As he went to pray for Danniebelle, he felt God say, ***"She's done...she's done."***

God was there to take Danniebelle Home.

At 5:30 pm on December 28, 2000, Danniebelle Hall entered into the gates of Heaven. No longer was her body in pain. Now she was completely renewed, with both legs. Pastors Andrae and Sandra Crouch were among those in the room. The song "The Best Gets Better" was playing in the background.

There were two homegoing services. A private service for the family was held at South Bay Community Church. A public service was held at the Center of Hope Community Church in Oakland, California, pastored by the late Earnestine Cleveland-Reems, with Pastor Yvette Flunder and Pastor

Carol Houston officiating. Bishop Walter Hawkins gave the invocation, followed by the Old Testament and New Testament readings by Elder Sandra Crouch and Pastor Brondon Reems.

The music was beautiful. It was like a huge Gospel fest. The Jones Sisters, (Paula, and Cynthia) recounted their childhood in Pittsburgh, Pennsylvania. The original Danniebelles (Paula, Jimmye, Phyllis, and honorary member, Shirley Miller), recounted their days as the Danniebelles. Andrae Crouch and the Disciples gave smashing renditions of signature songs many have come to identify with Danniebelle, such as "Soon and Very Soon," and "Take Me Back." When they sang "Tell Them," one could hear Danniebelle singing her part.

Jessy Dixon, Edwin, Walter and Tramaine Hawkins, Shirley Miller, Reba Rambo, BeBe Winans, and more were at the homecoming celebration...fit for a Queen! She is wearing her crown.

I CAME TO LET THEM KNOW

Danniebelle Reflects...

Have you ever stopped to think about what might have happened had God not intervened on your behalf at some crucial point in your life? What if things had gone the other way? Is He Lord of all the kingdoms of your heart? Have you confessed all? Have you said an eternal, "Yes!" All he wants to hear is yes! Eternally, unconditionally, absolutely..."Yes, Lord!"

Yes...until every fiber of your being resounds with "Yes Lord!"

You know that gentle tugging inside you that invades every area of your life? When you're eating, and even while you're sleeping, your spirit man does not sleep. Somewhere inside, you can sense what you'll come to know, introduced as the Holy Spirit, prodding you to the place that God had in His mind when He made you.

The Holy Spirit has no gun in your back, and yet He does, in the sense that He is on a mission from God. Oh, He'll let you have it your way until you come to the end of yourself and say, "I surrender." Hands up. Arms not just in a halfway elevation, but hands raised high above your head in total surrender.

Sometimes it takes a lifetime to come to this place. Sometimes it is in an instant. Sometimes you're lying in a hospital bed with nowhere else to go but to the Lord. You might be surrounded by friends, but somehow you realize you've got to get alone with God. A one-on-one kind of thing. Just tell him, "Yes! I'm yours."

Tell me what you want me to do. Right now, all I want to do is to be completely yours.

Whichever, however, whatever, whomever...

Give him the "Yes!" He wants to hear. The kind that resounds from the tip of your toenails to the end of every follicle on your head. Now you're ready to begin to live!

~Danniebelle

THE PRAYER OF SALVATION

Would you like to surrender your life to Christ and give God your yes? I invite you to pray this prayer of salvation with me. "Father God, I humbly come before Your throne asking You to forgive me of my sins. Your Word says in Romans 10:9-10, "if thou shalt confess with thy mouth the Lord Jesus, and shalt believe in thine heart that God hath raised him from the dead, thou shalt be saved." I believe Jesus Christ died for my sins, and because of His sacrifice, I offer my life to be used by You. *Teach me how to follow You. Guide my footsteps, open up my understanding, teach me what to say and do.* In Jesus' name, Amen.

~Cynthia

Look Mommy, I finished cleaning up my room!

Acknowledgements

Lest I forget, let me just mention a few names of those who have impacted my life (besides my own family). All of them are great people of God, and each, in their own way, has contributed, imparted, and made deposits in my life:

Elder Benjamin Scott, Sister Essie Scott, Elder Timothy McKnight, Mother Anna McKnight, Sister Tennis Smith, Sister Beulah Smith, Elder Eugene Cobb, Al Hopson, Al Belton, Andrae' Crouch, Sandra Crouch, Bob Osterman, Harold Brinkley, Ernestine Cleveland Reems, Carolyn Harrell, Archie and Claudette Dennis, Jimmye Jackson, Shirley Miller, Maxine Goodrich, Dora Taylor, Yvette Flunder, Corletta Harris-Vaughn, Bill Maxwell, Rowena Edwards, Phyllis St. James, Michael Brown, Paulette Goodall, Gloria Smallwood, Pastor Dorrough, Pastor and Sister John & Diana P. Cherry, Pastor Leonard Lucas, Ella Bogan, Pastor Clifford & Pastor Denise Turner, Niecy Dennis, Leo & Carolyn Gilman, Dottie Swafford, Charles & Cheryl Phillips, my babies, Billy and Boosie Gaines, my son Melvin Sanders, and another son Marvin Matthews, his wife, Rainey.

~Danniebelle

Thank you to my husband, Lance, my soulmate and dream facilitator.

Thank you, Charlotte and Charles, for your endless encouragement. Love your "Sittle Lister"

Thank you to my mother's remaining living siblings, "6,7, and 8"—Aunt Cindy, Auntie P, and Uncle Sam. I love you so very much.

A HUGE thank you to those that took the time to share their stories with me about my mother: The late Al Belton, Alfonzo Freeman, Babbie Mason, Beverly Caesar Sherrod, Bili Thedford, Bill & Judy Dodson, Bill Maxwell, Billy Gaines, Carl McGregor, Carol Houston, Charisse Fontes, Christal Roberts, Damian Bloomfield, Daryll Lewis, Ed & James Udell, Evie Karlsson, Fletch Wiley, Gregory Jones, Hadley Hockensmith, Harlan Rogers, Howard McCrary, Janice Williams, James Felix, Jeanne Gossett Halsey, Jeremiah Murphy, Jimmy & Michael Neubel, Jimmye Jackson, Joey Nardone, Kathy Hazzard, Kevin & Jan Craik, Lillie Knauls, Marvin Matthews, Michael Brown, Naomy Tallon, Nicky Cruz, Pamela Bates, Perry Morgan, Phyllis Swisher, Rainey Matthews, Reba Rambo, Rebecca Matthews, Richard Smallwood, Rowena Trim, Selwyn Collins, Scott Wesley Brown, Sheila Robinson, the late Shelley Lott, Shirley Miller, Pastor Emeritus Stanley Long, Dr. Teresa Hairston, Tim Dillinger-Curenton, Wintley Phipps, Yvette Flunder.

~Cynthia

www.ingramcontent.com/pod-product-compliance
Lightning Source LLC
Chambersburg PA
CBHW070343010526
44119CB00029B/416/J